Dash Diet Summ

If you are tired of trying every diet out there and never losing the weight, then the answer is finally here. The Dash Diet is the answer to your weight loss issues and it's based on healthy principles so you know it works. The best part is that when you read *"Learn How to Lose Weight Fast with Dash Diet Detox, Cleansing Diet, Glycemic Index Free Dash Diet Healthy Recipes! Lose 1 Pound Per Week! And Keep It Off! Free Mediterranean Diet Recipes!"* you learn all you ever needed to know.

This is an eBook that dives deep into not only the parameters of the Dash Diet, but also helps you to think of how to apply it to your everyday life. It helps you to understand how this diet works, but more importantly what sets it apart from everything else you have ever tried. You will learn more about yourself by reading this book and going through the journey than you ever imagined!

The Dash Diet was developed to help patients with hypertension and it was found that it also helped with long term and lasting weight loss. You can feel good about the platform of this diet as it was developed by medical professionals. The book takes you through the basics, shows you how to eat within this plan, and how to set up a healthy lifestyle to make it all work.

There is much more to weight loss than simply changing what you eat—but this book helps you with the nutrition component and so much more. You will learn what your problems may have been in the past, and how to actually solve them. By reading through this eBook you will know what it takes to lose the weight and keep it off, and you can use the platform of the Dash Diet easily and effectively. This is a good read and a helpful way to take the weight off once and for all!

"Healthy citizens are the greatest asset any country can have." **—Winston Churchill**

Table Of Content:

Introduction

Why Have Previous Weight Loss Attempts Failed?

How Can You Ensure That You Lose The Weight and Keep It Off This Time?

The Elements of a Healthy Lifestyle

The Importance of Goal Setting In Your Weight Loss Success

Adapting To a Positive Mindset and Using It For Ultimate Success

What Is The Dash Diet?

How Can This Solution Help You To Take The Weight Off For Good?

How Is This Diet Different Than Other Fads or Trends Out There?

How Can You Adapt This To Your Own Life?

Learning to Prepare For and Proactively Make This Diet Work In Your Lifestyle

Getting Rid Of The Wrong Foods and The Bad Habits

Making Changes For True and Long Lasting Weight Loss

Staying Focused and Committed To a Program That Really Works In Your Future

Conclusion

Bonus Offer Page (Detox Info with Free Recipes)

UPDATED ENHANCED EDITION! ADDITIONAL CHAPTERS ADDED!

Bonus Chapter (Detox Info)

Bonus Chapter (Glycemic Index Explained)

Few Healthy Herbs and Spices

Few Recipes

Dedication

Dedicated to you, my dear reader and to your healthy habits. It is our sincere intention in writing this book to help you achieve your optimal health.

Copyright Notice

All rights reserved in accordance with the Copyrights, Designs and Patents Act 1988. No part of this book may be reproduced in any form or by any electronic or mechanical means including information storage and retrieval system without permission from the author(s) and publisher, except by a reviewer who may quote brief passages in a review. Any person who carries out any unauthorized act in relation to this publication may be liable to criminal prosecution and civil claims for damages.
Publisher: Healthy Life Naturally
Author: Shawn Chhabra
Co-Author: Milo E Newton

Legal Disclaimer

This book is not intended to treat, diagnose or prescribe. Author, Publishers, Editors, and all other contributors have provided this material for entirely educational purposes. Use(s) of this information is entirely the responsibility of those who choose to apply this information for their personal health and wellbeing. This information is not intended as prescription, prognosis or diagnosis for any disease or illness, and should not be used as a replacement for any medical treatment you may currently be undergoing. It is not intended to substitute the medical expertise and advice of your primary health care provider. We encourage you to discuss any decisions about treatment or care with your health care provider.

The mention of any product, service, or therapy is not an endorsement by the publisher and its affiliates. The information provided is solely the opinion of the individual(s) and is, again, for educational purposes only. Application of information provided without supervision of a licensed medical doctor is done so at the individuals own risk.

Introduction

Losing weight is not an easy thing to do, and so many of us struggle with it throughout our lives. Just thinking about diets, deprivation, and previously failed attempts to lose the weight and keep it off can be depressing and stressful. Though the weight may have come on fairly easily depending on your phase of life or lifestyle itself, taking it off may not come quite as easily. That is all true until now!

The key to successful weight loss is to have a program that will help to not only get you going but to support you along the way. A solid weight loss program should be based in healthy concepts and always work within parameters that never put your body in danger. Though the many fads and trends out there may sound good in theory, they certainly aren't meant to help you in the long term once you try them out.

There Is No Quick Answer — You Have To Work For It

We all want to lose weight, and we want to do it quickly and easily. It may be unsettling to think that there is something about your lifestyle that you will need to change, but this is the reality of the situation. You never want to be drastic in your approach because these are the types of habits that not only aren't going to be something that you can't keep up with, but they are also extremely unhealthy at the core.

Sure the many trends, fads, and diets out there may sound good on paper, but how easy are they to take on for the long term? When it comes to calorie cutting, logging every bite of food you eat, or deprivation in any form, this is not something that you are going to keep up with forever more. Not only that, but these methods are often intended to help you lose weight initially, but will leave you feeling unhealthy and hungry as time goes on.

What makes the Dash Diet such a successful program is the fact that it is based on truly healthy concepts? This is a program that was developed to help a specific health condition, and then the implications of this were found to be extremely helpful for weight loss in the process. So you know that what you are getting into is well founded and that you are going to benefit from it in so many ways.

The Key To Long Term Weight Loss Is Here
This book is going to show you why there are good sugars and bad sugars. You are going to learn that what AND how you eat really matters. You are going to see that it really comes down to creating and maintaining a healthy lifestyle. You are also going to see that the power to make change comes from within you, and that if you want it bad enough you can achieve that long term weight loss that you have always dreamed about.

Though you may feel frustrated in previous weight loss attempts and marked failures, this time will be different. You are going to learn not only what it takes to lose weight and keep it off, but you will also get insight into your own habits. You will see what didn't work for you in the past and more importantly WHY it didn't work for you. This is a very broad approach and therefore quite informative as you work towards the success that you have always dreamed of.

It's time to cast aside what you thought you knew about weight loss, and to learn what really works. It's not just about adapting to the right program such as this, but also learning precisely what went wrong in the past. Not only understanding what you may have done wrong, but also what the diets that you've used in the past didn't give you. This is a learning process and this is the beginning of a long and educational journey!

So come into this weight loss journey with an open mind, find and embrace your inner strength and confidence, and be willing to commit to a program that is going to help you and support you in the long term. Though you may have felt frustration in the past, it's time to really celebrate the transformation that you have always wanted. This is how you lose weight and enjoy success well into your future — so let's get started!

Why Have Previous Weight Loss Attempts Failed?

It's fair to feel skeptical when it comes to losing weight, even when you hear that it's a healthy and proven program such as the Dash Diet. Though you feel as though you've heard it all before, this time really will be different and you will soon understand why. To be able to be successful in the future however, you need to learn from previous mistakes. There are some valid reasons as to why previous weight loss attempts failed, and it's time to understand them.

Many people have a tendency to blame themselves when the diets that they've used don't work. Sure there is a certainly level of accountability that comes with weight loss in general, and more than likely you may need to change a certain aspect of what you are doing. The truth is though that to get to long term weight loss you also need a program that is intended for the long term. You need a framework that keeps your health and your true and lasting success in mind, and you have finally found the right one.

It's About Learning From Past Mistakes and Knowing How to Focus Moving Forward

Many people will tell you that slow and steady wins the race, and that's partially true. You will see that the Dash Diet will help you to not only take off weight that stays off, but that you can lose up to a pound a week if you stick with the program. This is not the case with anything else out there and that's why you need to see what went wrong in the past. Don't take this as an admission of guilt or anything to feel bad about, but rather enjoy becoming educated and ensuring that you don't head down the wrong path again.

So while you don't want to dwell in the past, you do want to understand what went wrong. Even if you feel as though you have tried every single diet out there, you will find that there are a few common threads that prevented you from losing weight. While you will need to change your lifestyle moving forward, you will also see that it wasn't just about you failing the diets — in most instances the reality is that the diets failed you!

What Went Wrong and How Can You Keep It From Happening Again?
It's hard to stare in the face of perceived failure and try to learn something from it. We all have a hard time admitting that something went wrong, but look at it as a way of being successful now and into the future. Here are some very real reasons why previous weight loss attempts ended in disaster.

- The diet was only ever intended to help you lose weight quickly:

    So many diets out there were only ever intended to help you to get a jump start on your weight loss efforts. They obviously don't advertise themselves that way and so you are instantly disappointed when the weight loss comes to a halt.
    Much of what you lose on such diets is water weight and therefore the progress won't continue on for very long. Any time you greatly restrict your intake or drastically cut your calories you are going to lose weight. This is not only an unhealthy way to go about it, but you will find that it's also not something that will keep you going for very long.
    Many diets take the approach of lose it quickly now and worry about the rest later — and this will always leave you feeling disappointed and more than likely cause you to gain the weight back as you move along.

- You were never going to be able to keep up with the measures in the long term:

    How long are you going to be able to avoid an entire food group? How long will you keep up with tracking every bite of food that you take? How long can you possibly deprive yourself and eat only a very restrictive number of calories? The truth is that any of these drastic or extreme measures that so many diets are founded on will never get you to where you want to be. Think about the premise of a given diet and then ask yourself if you can see doing this six months or even a year from now. If you answer "no" then this is not a diet to be taken on because it's only meant for the short term.
    So while you have been so hard on yourself for failed attempts at weight loss in the past, the truth is that these diets and the methods that they enlist were never going to be there to help support you in long term and lasting weight loss. Take that in and you will start to take all of the responsibility and blame off of yourself!

- You felt deprived, hungry, and were likely taking on a very unhealthy method to lose the weight:

    Here's the thing to remember — you are only going to allow yourself to feel hungry and therefore deprived for so long. We all start out with the best of intentions but as time goes on and your body naturally feels hunger, you are going to start to look for whatever you can find.
    So as many diets out there focus on limiting yourself in an often drastic manner, you are going to end up giving into temptation. Part of this is up to you to learn will power but you should also note that a good diet never makes you feel deprived.

The Dash Diet will never put you in a situation based on extremes and certainly will help you to create healthy habits for now and the future. That keeps you from the highs and lows that you are probably so familiar with by now.

- It only focused on one particular aspect of weight loss:

In order to work towards true weight loss you need to consider every factor that will contribute to this. That means that you need a truly healthy lifestyle to support you in your efforts. Sure the foods that you eat are a big part of it, but it's also about the way in which you eat them.
It's also about the big picture and that's a point that is often lost on so many people. You need to engage in a challenging fitness regimen, get plenty of rest, and learn to manage your stress. In the end it's about taking care of yourself as a whole rather than just adjusting your calorie count each day.

How Can You Ensure That You Lose The Weight and Keep It Off This Time?

So what's going to make this time different? So many of us start with the best of intentions and yet feel that anxiety due to previous failed attempts. We want to lose weight, we want to remain committed, we want the best out of life, and yet we've felt that pain of disappointment so many times over. So how can you ensure that this time really works?
First and foremost you are working within the framework of a valuable and proven diet program with the Dash Diet. That in and of itself will provide the important foundation required to help you to lose the weight and keep it off. Sure you have to commit to it and follow the guidelines given, but knowing that you have a supportive and proven foundation helps matters tremendously.
You Play a Major Role In Your Ability To Be Successful
You also want to be sure that your attitude and dedication is present more so than ever before. We have seen by now that we didn't fail the diet but they failed us, and so that knowledge is very powerful. There is some accountability on our part though to ensure that we don't just give into this and neglect to put ourselves into the program wholeheartedly.

If you want to achieve weight loss success and maintain those results then you need to be committed to this program in every sense of the word. You have to believe in yourself and what you are doing, you have to be ready to take on the hard work and do whatever it takes, and you also have to be willing to change your lifestyle and get rid of the obstacles or bad habits that may have held you back in the past.
Now is the time for change! In order to get that change and to achieve the body and life that you have always wanted for yourself, you have to get yourself there. You now have the foundation of a great program, but the rest is up to you. In order to lose all of the weight and keep it off for good you have to be ready and willing to take on the components presented to you and keep working at it your entire life through. This is how you achieve and hold onto true and lasting weight loss success!

All Of The Factors For Long Term Success Are Yours

You've learned what went wrong in the past and now it's time to make it right. The diet failed you but learning accountability will help you tremendously as you move forward. So start by understanding the factors that contribute to your success and what will ensure that you get everything you want out of your journey this time.

- You are committed physically, mentally, and emotionally:

    This is more than just a physical commitment though that is certainly part of it. You do need to commit through the physical in your workouts and your food preparation, amongst other factors. You must also commit in every other sense or your progress will be limited.

You have to maintain a confidence and inner strength that tells you that you CAN do this. You have to be ready to take on the obstacles or challenges and use will power and determination to get you through. This will help you to break free of previously harmful patterns and ensure that you remain committed even when things get tough.

You are going to have good days and bad days and it is that determination and commitment that will help you to persevere even if you have challenging moments. Throw yourself in this process and journey in every sense of the word and it will make all the difference in the world!

- You are using a program that is proven and for the long term such as the Dash Diet:

You've tried every other method, diet, program, fad, and trend out there and felt disappointed. This time is different because of the foundation and program that you are using, and that will make a huge difference as well. The Dash Diet has been around for years and offering a unique and well balanced solution to weight loss along the way.

This is a program that is focused on good health and therefore the benefits are immeasurable. Though this diet was devised to help those with high blood pressure, it has helped so many people to achieve their weight loss goals.

You should feel good about the healthy component that ensures that you don't just lose weight, but that you do so in an appropriate manner that will equal up to long term success. This is a medically sound diet program that will always put you first and will be the foundation that helps you through the long term.

- You learn from past mistakes and find motivation within them:

  We all have problematic dieting behavior, obstacles, patterns, and challenges that have held us back in the past. To be able to move forward you have to learn from those mistakes. It may have been temptations in the way of certain foods or falling off track around vacations or holidays, but you find a way to stay committed no matter what.
  Whatever you have done wrong in the past, it's time to face it head on. We all make mistakes and we all have problem areas that can hold us back, but it's about facing them and using them to make us stronger. It may not always be easy to admit these faults, but in the end they will make you stronger and more committed.

- You change your lifestyle for the better and don't just fix one component:

  While other diets focus only on changing the foods that you eat, this is a diet that's truly about the big picture. You are not just changing the food component but so much more through a lifestyle overhaul. If you can adjust to that mindset and really understand that it's about taking care of yourself, then you will enjoy long term success.

When you get rid of the bad habits and replace them with good clean and healthy living, then you learn what it means to truly take care of yourself. Then and only then are you creating a platform by which you can lose weight, but where you can also improve your health as well. This is revolutionary not just to your ability to lose weight, but also in your focus as you move forward and start to really enjoy life in this healthy new way.

The Elements of a Healthy Lifestyle

More than likely you have heard so much about a healthy lifestyle and the necessity of this. So what exactly does this mean? How can you make improvements and be sure to live your best life and what exactly does that entail? Hopefully you are already using certain measures that help to keep you healthy, but there is always room for improvement and that's a good place to start.

A healthy lifestyle should be your natural platform because it helps to keep you your best. This is what leads you towards good health now and well into your future. Beyond that though you will also find that a healthy lifestyle is instrumental in your ability to lose weight and keep it off. These are balanced and proper habits that will lead you to being your best, and a big factor in that is maintaining a healthy weight range. So the benefits are countless!

So Many Different Factors Working Together In Harmony
A healthy lifestyle is much more than people think it is though and this is where things can get rather deceiving. Sure proper nutrition through good food is part of a healthy lifestyle, but it doesn't end there. You will find that there are many elements that make up a healthy lifestyle and that each of them is equally important. Each these work in harmony and when they are, then you are at your very best.

You will find that you aren't really your best without each component at work. So that means that it's about nutrition, but also fitness, rest, and stress management as examples. When you can look at the big picture you see that each component is a requirement and when they are working together simultaneously then you can enjoy really great things for yourself. You can feel just how instrumental each factor is when you are doing everything just right!

You can't get to true weight loss and enjoy the best health benefits without every factor playing a part in your life. So it's time to get healthy and work towards a long term solution that will help to prevent medical problems, keep your health intact, and always ensure that you are your very best — this is what a healthy lifestyle is all about!

These Are The Elements That Make You Your Healthiest and Best

Though we tend to look at weight loss as only about the foods that we eat or even the exercise that we take on, it's much more than that. In order to lose weight and maintain these results, it's essential to keep a keen eye on the healthiest habits possible. This is what will help to keep you your very best and ensure that you not only lose weight, but feel great in the long term besides that.

So let's focus in on the various components that equal weight loss success and enjoy how each component can benefit us.

- Proper and Balanced Nutrition:

    You will learn more about how the Dash Diet specifically defines the right foods to eat, but suffice it to say this is all about proper nutrition. This is about cutting out the processed foods and instead focusing on whole and natural foods that offer you key nutrients. That's what balanced nutrition is all about — you will lose weight but you will also feel great energy as you eat well.

Balanced nutrition means that you include foods from each food group and that you focus on how to get the most out of them. You want to know exactly where your food comes from, what it's made up of, and be sure that it doesn't contain a whole list of ingredients that you can't even pronounce.

When you eat in this way you are not only going to lose weight, but you are also going to feel so much better as well. You will be able to turn to food for vitamins and minerals and enjoy what balanced eating is really meant to be. This is how you get to long term weight loss, and you also enjoy some wonderful health benefits in the process.

- Eating the Right Foods in the Right Way:

It's not just about WHAT you eat, but also about HOW you eat them. This is a distinction that so many people don't recognize and it could be contributing to the weight loss and weight gain cycle. So many people have a tendency to skip meals as they feel it gives them an edge in calorie cutting. The problem is that you then tend to overeat at the next meal and the up and down cycle continues.

The way that you were intended to eat was smaller meals more frequently. This ensures that you never skip meals, never overeat, and also keep your body fueled all day long. This is a healthy practice to get into and ensures that you stay on track throughout the course of the entire day.

When you can combine food groups you make for a truly powerful mini meal. Aim for eating these smaller meals about every 3-4 hours, or at least 5-6 mini meals throughout your day. Sure you are going to have to plan for them, but this is a great way to stay satisfied and to ensure you take in what you need all day long.

- Creating and Maintaining a Challenging Fitness Regimen:

    So many diet plans out there talk only about the food portion of losing weight. Sure the foods that you eat play a major role in things, but so too does the fitness component. Without fitness you may lose weight initially, but more than likely will hit a plateau and have an inability to continue the weight loss process. You must commit to a challenging fitness regimen that keeps your body guessing. That means that you want to incorporate a great deal of variety into your routine, for when the body is guessing is when it is transforming. You also want to combine cardio and strength training as this will help to burn away the fat, but add in the muscle tone that you are after.
    Try to aim for working out at least 5 times a week and continue to challenge yourself so that your body is always responding to get you the results that you are after. This is how true body transformation occurs!

- Getting Plenty of Rest:

    Believe it or not, how much rest you get within a day can play heavily on your ability to lose weight or not. When you are sleep deprived your willpower is down and this is when you make bad choices. There have been studies too that have linked sleep deprivation to weight gain, and so it all naturally fits together.

What this all means is that getting plenty of rest is yet another essential way of taking care of yourself. This is how you rejuvenate and if you aren't getting proper sleep then it's hard to commit to fitness or healthy eating or any other factors.

All aspects of a healthy lifestyle are undoubtedly important and proper sleep is no exception. You should be striving for about 7-8 hours every night and make this a priority as this is when your body is repairing, rejuvenating, and preparing for the next day.

- Learning To Manage Your Stress:

If you don't already know it, stress can play a major role in your ability to lose weight. We all know that stress isn't good for you, but it has a direct impact on you gaining weight or losing weight. When your body feels under stress, it can often release certain hormones that contribute to belly fat. This is reason enough to try to really work through natural stress management. Stress will wear you down and make you more likely to make improper health choices. It will also make you eat more in many cases, and the terrible cycle continues. So if you needed a healthy way to learn to manage your stress, let this be the catalyst to work through this issue. If you are trying to lose weight, stress will always work against you!

- Getting Rid of the Bad Habits:

All of the bad habits that you probably justify are contributing to you gaining weight or having trouble losing it. Bad habits such as skipping meals or binging, smoking, drinking excessive caffeine or alcohol, a sedentary lifestyle, and so many more are all directly or indirectly linked to weight gain.

If you are really serious about losing weight, the Dash Diet will be the program to get you there. The problem is that you are going to have to ditch the bad habits once and for all and really work to create a clean and truly healthy lifestyle. These habits are holding you back, keeping you from progress, and ensuring that you are certainly not your very best at all.

The Importance of Goal Setting In Your Weight Loss Success

You may have used goal setting at some point in your life. Maybe you have thought about it but never really sat down to consider how beneficial goal setting could be in your life. So many of us have incorporated goals into our professional life, but then have a hard time figuring out how to make it work within our personal life. The truth is that goal setting can be the one catalyst that helps you in so many areas of your life, particularly in weight loss.

In order to be successful in anything you need to have a path and a plan to get there. This may not always be easy, but anything worthwhile is worth working for. That means that goal setting may be the one thing that can help you to capture your thoughts and ideas and create a plan that will lead you towards success. This does require some soul searching and jotting everything down, but it will be well worth the effort in the end.

This Will Make The Difference and Head You Down The Path Towards Success

Goal setting plays a pivotal role within weight loss and you will really enjoy the journey as it comes together. Rather than just saying you want to lose "X" number of pounds, you create a path that leads you to that long term goal through the shorter term ones. This is about true accountability and about taking control of your destiny through the effort that you put in.

If you perform this exercise correctly then you see firsthand how goal setting works. Not only can you start to see things come together, but you can also decipher what's working and more importantly what's not working. It's only as good as the thought and effort that you put forth and so this has to be something that you keep up with. Keeping your goals visible and then checking your progress helps you to decide upon the right path to move forward with.

When you combine a great program such as the Dash Diet with proper goal setting then there is literally no stopping you. This is a great way to cut through the clutter and past disappointments and really remain focused on what you are doing all of this for. This takes the hard work and really heads it in the right direction!

Here's How Goal Setting Works At Its Best

Whether you have used goal setting in the past or you are starting fresh, there are certain aspects you should always consider within the goals that you set. In order to make this work for your weight loss and to really achieve what you are after, there are a few considerations that will make your path more beneficial.

Here are the important aspects that help to make goal setting work for you and lead you towards true success.

- Short term goals will create the path to get you to your long term ultimate goals:

    Everyone has a long term goal in mind and that's what we tend to focus so much of our time on. Though long term goals such as losing a certain number of pounds are important, it's also about much more than that. The long term goal is something that you work towards and strive for, but the shorter term goals are the ones that will help you to get there.

So by all means set your long term goal such as losing so much weight or being in a certain size, but then think of how you can get there. The shorter term goals can include losing a certain amount of weight in a month, hitting the gym a certain number of weeks, or even trying a new healthy food each week.

The short term goals are what help to keep you motivated as you reach them each time, and they give you a sense check of what is working and what's not to keep you on track towards the ultimate long term goal.

- Make your goals tangible and measurable:

It's crucial to your success to throw numbers or measurable factors at your goals. Anyone can say that they want to lose weight, but how much? What sort of timeframes do you want to center things around? How are you going to get to these goals and how can you measure that progress?

Good examples include working out five times a week, cooking for yourself six times a week, trying one new exercise each week, losing two inches within a month, etc. The more measurable you can make your goals the more tangible they become. This is when you can really focus in on measuring what is working for you. This all helps you to be accountable and for you to see a clear path of what's working and what's not in your life.

- Keep your goals visible so that you see them often and are reminded of their purpose:

Goals are no good if you don't keep reviewing them, so remember that. You need to post your goals that you write down in a visible place such as the bathroom mirror that you are going to see every single day. This is a great reminder of what you are working towards and what's going to help to get you there.
You need to revisit those goals and really keep them visible always. Maybe you bring a copy of them everywhere you go to cement your commitment to the process. It's a long journey but when you see the goals that you have written down before you then you can remember what it's all about and how you intend to get there.

- Track progress and be sure that the goals make you accountable:

Let these goals instill a certain sense of accountability and then they are working their best. Be sure to revisit the goals often and track your progress. Then you can see what is working well and continue on – you can also change up the elements that aren't working well for you.
Try to aim for even once a week to revisit your goals and then change up the factors that aren't working well. This makes you accountable and helps to reshape your path every so often. This is the type of commitment that will keep you strong and ensure that you use goal setting to really help you to make some major progress in losing weight and being your healthiest.

Adapting To a Positive Mindset and Using It For Ultimate Success

As you think through previous weight loss attempts you now see what went wrong. In many cases there was a lot that went wrong, and that's all part of the learning process. You see that the diets that you utilized were flawed. You saw that it was about making certain changes within your life and therefore creating a new and better lifestyle for yourself. You also need to understand that adapting to a positive mindset is an important part of the process as well.

This is one area that so many people tend to skip over. They assume that positive thinking and a good attitude are a "nicety" but not a necessity. This couldn't be further from the truth! If you are going through the motions but don't really believe in what you are doing then it's all for nothing. If you don't embrace the process mentally and invest the right attitude into the actions, then you are never going to get anywhere. That's why a positive mindset is going to really help to guide you to success.

When you think about how many things are impacted by your mindset and your attitude, it's no wonder that this is a very necessary component for true and lasting success. Your attitude and beliefs guide your willpower, your abilities, your confidence level, and the actual effort that you put into the process. If you don't really believe in what you are doing on any level, then it's never going to work for you. Inevitably you will get bored, complacent, or just give up because you feel like you aren't getting anywhere.
The way that you feel and view the weight loss journey is going to shape everything you do and really play into how successful you are. Think of previous attempts — at some point in time you gave up and stopped caring about what you were doing. You either hit a plateau, gave into temptations, or had a difficult time in overcoming a challenge. It was at that point where you gave up and stopped feeling good about what you were doing that things shifted towards the negative.
If you go into the journey recognizing that you are going to hit rough spots and have bad days, then you are being realistic. If you can persevere with a good attitude to get you through those rough patches then you will inevitably overcome what held you back in the past. It is that positive mindset and that proactive attitude that will really come in handy. That's what makes the difference — when you feel good about what you are doing and can stay in touch with that positivity then you have a greater chance at long term success.

A Positive Mindset Makes All The Difference In The World
The way that you view the world, how you feel about things, and what you do with yourself are all tied into attitude. Your confidence, your willpower, your motivation, and your approach are all tied together and that's why your mindset is so crucial.

If you want to be successful then you must realize that this is a major factor within your ability to do so. You will not only enjoy the journey so much more, but you are also setting yourself up to do so much better. Your mindset, your attitude, and the way that you view all of this is critical and here are the reasons why and how you get it to work for you.

- You have to BELIEVE in what you are doing:

    If you don't actually believe in what you are doing but are simply going through the motions, this is not going to fare well for you. Not only are you going to feel miserable with everything you are doing, but you are not going to get the results that you want.
    Your mindset gives you the power to make it through the rough days and to persevere. Your attitude can help you to remain motivated and strong, even when it may be challenging. If you just go through the motions and never really feel it deep down, then you are not going to stick with it for very long.
    Not only that but you are going to fall off track much easier, give up, or simply hit a plateau because you are not giving it your all. So though you may have thought of attitude as a "nicety" before, now you see that believing in what you are doing really is important.

- You have to find and embrace confidence and inner strength:

    You can be your own worst enemy or your best supporter, the choice is up to you. When you find that inner confidence and strength that dwells deep down you unlock a key to your happiness. You can feel good about what you are doing because you feel good about yourself, and that matters tremendously in the end.

To be confident is to be self assured, and this will help you with every single aspect of this program. So as you think through your approach to make this time truly different it must be taken on with great confidence in your abilities and determination to make this work.

You are stronger than you give yourself credit for and when you can get in touch with that then you can make this work. A weight loss program is only as good as the effort that you put forth into it. If you don't feel confident and strong then you are not going to stick with it.

You are going to need confidence to help you to stay with the program and to make it through the little challenges that arise along the way. Confidence will also help you to get to where you want to be and enjoy the journey for all that its worth!

- When you feel positive and motivated, then you can keep working towards progress:

You know how it goes when you have those days where everything just seems to fall in line and work well? That is positive energy at its best and that is a critical part of the weight loss process. So though you may underestimate the power of positive thinking, consider how great it is when it's at work in your life. This holds especially true within weight loss because that positivity can really take you to great places. You're positive and therefore motivated and that gives you that little push to take on challenges like never before. You are more effective in your workouts, you are more ambitious in your cooking, and you know what it means to put all of the guidelines together in one cohesive manner.

You don't let the little things get to you nor do you let stress in life overtake you. No longer do you give into that negative voice in your head because you feel great through and through and are sure that you are heading down the path to lead you towards success — this really works well all together!

- A positive mindset will keep you strong in the face of adversity or challenges:

No matter what challenges may face you along the way, positive thinking will give you everything you need to overcome it. You have more willpower, strength, confidence, and drive to overcome a temptation or a bad day.
You get back on track quickly, ignore the negative thoughts, and really push forward to make lasting weight loss a true reality. This is what it means to be successful and to make your attitude work FOR you and not against you anymore.

What Is The Dash Diet?

So you understand by now why your previous diet attempts didn't work. You see firsthand that the efforts that you were taking on were never going to lead you to long term success. You have also probably learned a bit about yourself and what you personally did wrong in your past weight loss attempts. The learning process is only just beginning, but you may be starting to ask yourself "what is the Dash Diet all about anyhow?"

Yes you understand that this is a weight loss program that will set you up for success, but how? You see the problem with so many fads, trends, and diets out there, and now you want to understand just what makes the Dash Diet so different. Many people who have considered the Dash Diet have sat exactly where you do right now and have wondered just what makes this such a helpful program and sets it apart from so many other programs.

Know That This Time Will Be Different But Understand Why

It's fine to be skeptical and even healthy to consider all of your facts. Yes the Dash Diet truly is different and it really will provide the structure to lead you to long term weight loss, but you do want to be sure that you understand how that works. This is all about setting that all important positive mindset. In order to be successful you need to understand what you are doing and why, and so gaining insight into the ins and outs of the Dash Diet is an important first step in establishing that core foundation.

The Dash Diet is going to take you to where you want to go, and it will do so keeping your health at the forefront. The beauty of this diet is that it wasn't even created for weight loss specifically and perhaps that's what makes it so successful. So tune into what this diet is all about and learn what makes this different than anything else you have tried. You are going to experience great things, and learning just why is the first and most important step of this journey — and what will make this all different for you this time around!

Why Is This So Very Different And What Makes It So Truly Effective?
The Dash diet was developed by medical professionals and that in and of itself sets it apart from other programs out there. You are not getting the opinion of somebody who tried to lose weight once, but rather the medically sound advice of those that know. You will benefit from the insight of what it takes to naturally lower hypertension and the results for weight loss have been proven over and over again.

So as you move forward and try to understand what the Dash diet is all about, here are some guidelines to help you get started and kick off this long term weight loss journey.

- A diet developed to help people control their hypertension:

    The original premise of the Dash diet came about to help people with hypertension. There was a strong belief that lowering elevated blood pressure levels could come through the foods that you eat, and that's why this diet was developed. It was found after the diet came to be and was tested against other studies that it could actually benefit weight loss as well.

So while the diet was put in place to help with hypertension, you can rest assured that it helps from a well thought out place. These are medically sound concepts that are developed to keep good health at the forefront. As you are lowering your blood pressure if that is an issue, you are also losing weight in the right way. This is how your body was intended to lose weight, and so it takes a natural and very well rounded approach to it from the start.

- A diet that is high in fruits, vegetables, and foods with key nutrients:

    One of the major focuses of the Dash Diet is to consume nutrient rich foods. That comes obviously from the most natural foods from the earth. So the focus here is on foods such as fruits and vegetables, lean proteins, whole grains, and good fats. This is the way that you are supposed to be eating and so natural weight loss evolves from this.
    You are giving your body what it needs, not only to lower blood pressure but also to lose weight and to get healthy. This is the type of eating that comes from the food pyramid by which you are eating using whole food categories that make for balanced nutrition. This is a slower approach to weight loss, but a lasting one that ensures that you eat and that you focus on the right foods at that.

- A program that focuses on lower fat consumption and elimination of substances such as sodium:

As you are focusing on eating all of the right foods, you are also ensuring that you get rid of all the wrong foods. The Dash Diet promotes lowering overall fat consumption, particularly saturated fat which has a close link to hypertension in the first place. Though you shouldn't be eating these foods anyhow, the Dash Diet sets up the parameters to ensure that you lower fat consumption overall.

This means no more fried foods, processed foods, foods that are high in additives, preservatives, or even sodium. All of these have direct links to elevated blood pressure levels and contribute to weight gain as well. You should be eliminating these things for good health, but as you do so you are also ensuring that you focus on calorie restriction in a healthy and effective manner. This is how you should be eating and these are the foods that you should avoid!

- A medically sound diet that is aimed at naturally lowering blood pressure, and also helps tremendously with lasting weight loss in the process:

  Focusing on key nutrients, fiber, and balanced and healthy eating is always going to be good for weight loss. The Dash diet doesn't promote losing weight through extreme measures, but rather using the structure of a healthy lifestyle with balanced and proper nutrition to get you there. This was developed to help lower blood pressure in a natural way and so you will enjoy weight loss as so many patients have throughout the years.

When so many diets out there are brought about without any health merit to them, the Dash Diet stands apart for the way it was devised. This is truly a medically sound diet that was intended to help with a specific health condition. Since it introduces healthy concepts that you should be focusing on, it helps you to achieve weight loss in the best way possible. So you can rest assured that the results that you will get will be long term and always keep your health as the main priority.

How Can This Solution Help You To Take The Weight Off For Good?

So you see what makes the Dash Diet different and what makes it such a successful program. Sometimes though we may see something right there before us, it doesn't quite sink in as part of our life. You do need to make the commitment and ensure that you are ready to take the necessary steps. The great thing to keep in mind and to keep reminding yourself of however is that this program can work and it will be the solution for you if you allow it to be.

So how are you going to welcome this solution in? How are you going to be sure that this time it really works for you? Though you may understand the framework of the Dash Diet, how can you be sure that you make this the time where you turn it all around. Sure a program such as this is excellent and based in truths that will help you to get to where you want to be. The only problem is that if you don't set up the parameters in your own life and with your own effort ,then the program will fail as will you.

This Program Plus Your Effort Equals Lasting Success

Knowing that the Dash Diet can make the difference and that it truly is for the long term makes it all possible. How can you make sure that you understand what makes this work and what can you do to create healthy habits around it? You have seen firsthand the power of positive thinking, goal setting, changing your ways, and creating a truly healthy lifestyle. So how can you then welcome in the Dash Diet and create a successful and lasting platform that really helps you to achieve long term weight loss?

It's easier than you might think but it's definitely going to require some serious effort on your part. Viewing the Dash Diet the right way and then making that connection back to what your role is within making this successful is key. Again remember that a long term weight loss solution such as the Dash Diet is only as good as the effort that you put into it. Yes this is a program that CAN and WILL work for you — however to be truly successful now and into the long term that means that you must make some changes along the way. Here we look at why this time will be successful and what it will take from you in conjunction with the Dash Diet to make it work once and for all!

This Is What Will Take You To The Next Step and Ensure Success Is Yours

Losing weight now and well into the long term will work with the Dash Diet. In order to take the weight off initially and keep the effort going until you reach maintenance though, you do need to keep a couple of things in mind. It's essential that you make the changes, follow the Dash Diet as it is presented, and really be ready to change your lifestyle as a whole rather than just one element of it.

So there are many reasons that the Dash Diet can help you to be successful and it centers around these concepts and these changes that you will make when you follow it. Here's how it works and why it's so effective.

- Out with the bad and in with the good:

    One of the fundamental concepts of the Dash Diet is that you get rid of some of the most toxic and therefore harmful substances when it comes to weight loss. Saturated fat, excess fat overall, sodium, and additives and preservatives all contribute to weight gain in the long term. The Dash Diet works to get rid of these and therefore helps you to lose weight the right way.
    As you are getting these bad and harmful substances out, you are welcoming in new and better ones to replace them. So you get rid of fried foods, processed foods, and excess sodium — but then you replace them with lean proteins, loads of fruits and vegetables and true whole grains. This is how you are intended to eat and making these changes will lead you to long term weight loss.
    The changes may be more gradual with weight loss than with extreme measures, but you know it will work because the weight will stay off for good. As you welcome in the new and better, you get rid of the bad that was always going to hold you back.

- It takes a slower but more long term approach to weight loss:

    Yet another key to success with such a program as the Dash Diet is the fact that it takes a slower and therefore healthier approach to weight loss. Since this was a diet that was intended to help people with hypertension, it was never solely about weight loss in the first place and that's a good thing overall.

When you focus only on measures tied to weight loss, they usually end up being the type to give you a jump start. Calorie reduction or deprivation for example are only helping you to fix one part of the problem and so the weight will come off very quickly at first, but then will end up packing back on as you move forward.
If it's not a long term approach then you can wrongfully be encouraged when the weight tends to come off quickly at first. You will often hit a plateau and the weight loss will come to a quick stop. When you use the long term approach of the Dash Diet you end up losing weight slower at first, but then it's consistent and you keep taking the weight off. You then get into healthier habits and are doing all the right things so that you can then adapt to this new lifestyle and keep the weight off for good. That's why this works!

- It assumes a healthy lifestyle as the foundation of it:

    This is a major difference and why the Dash Diet is going to work for you — it centers around a healthy lifestyle at the core. Not only are you focused on eating the right foods, but you are also getting rid of bad habits in the process such as excessive salt, eating too much red meat, and so on. You are also encouraged to work out and really take care of yourself for a healthy lifestyle at the core.

You learn good habits that are not only going to help you to lose weight and keep it off, but also will help you to get healthier. This is what a solid weight loss foundation is based off of and what creates a foundation for healthier, happier living that includes being at a healthy weight range. When you learn good healthy habits and how to properly take care of yourself, then you are transforming your body and asking it to change.

The right foods, some good exercise, and a lifestyle that supports long term weight loss will ensure that you keep the weight off for good — you are going to feel more energized and happier because you are making changes that really count for the better! While the rest of the diets out there have only ever focused on changing what you eat, the Dash Diet goes much further and really dives into what it means to transform your life, take the weight off and keep it off, and get into healthier habits so you know it works well.

How Is This Diet Different Than Other Fads or Trends Out There?

There are so many diets out there, and sometimes it's hard to decipher what really sets them all apart. The truth is that you need to really inspect each weight loss program closely to fully understand what makes it up. Though you may feel that at the core all diets are the same, there are some major differences that can lead you to success or failure. The Dash Diet is set apart from all the rest for a variety of reasons, and the most notable is the fact that it is not based on the most recent trend or fad.

The fact is that when you look at the landscape of all of the diets and weight loss programs out there, the vast majority of them are based on trends and fads. They are created for the "in the moment" type of weight loss trend that is passed down from the opinion of one to the masses. We all want to believe in them as they seem to be so reassuring and offer such promise for our ability to lose weight. We've seen by now though how this ends, and it's not well!

It's Easy To Be Swayed But You Need To Know Why Not To Be
Though you do understand what makes the Dash Diet so special by now, it's important to compare and contrast to really see the differences come to life. You may very well be tempted at some point, even while working through the Dash Diet, to give into the temptation of a "quick and easy promise" to weight loss. Not only is this harmful but it won't get you results, and so understanding the main differences is essential.

Though the many fads and trends out there may change over time for weight loss, they are all there to give you short term and very limited support. You may be enticed by their quick results that they assure you will come, but you know that you won't get what you want out of them.

When you compare to a diet such as the Dash Diet that is based on healthy principles and therefore long term results, you start to see that the path is clear. Beyond that though you do need to be mindful that these comparisons help to create the platform that makes up the Dash Diet and leads you to long term success with weight loss — this diet picks up where other diets leave off!

Comparing The Latest Trend With The Proven Dash Diet
So while you may understand the importance of a well founded weight loss program such as the Dash Diet, it can be quite helpful to compare to what you have done in the past. Then the next time that you are tempted or swayed to go to the method that seems so easy and seamless, you will understand why sticking with the proven program will always serve you well.

- It's based on truly healthy concepts that help to change your body:

    The latest fads and trends out there are based solely on how to lose weight quickly and have no real merit to them. There's a reason that the latest fad is constantly changing and that's because they are usually based upon opinion and the whim of some "expert" that isn't really educated in these matters.

That being said, when you turn to a program like the Dash Diet you can feel good that the foundation is all based on true health and medical concepts. Though you may feel that the trend is so tempting, recognize that the Dash Diet will always support you and leave you in the right state. The healthy concepts at the core of it are what lead you to long term success — and no trend can do that!

- It is intended to help you to lose weight slower, but to keep the weight off for the long term:

    Sure you may get faster results or see more weight come off initially using a fad, but how long will it last? So many of the diets out there will only ever help you to lose weight quickly but then the plateau comes along and your progress comes to a screeching halt. Losing weight slower is the way to go and a surefire way to ensure that the weight stays off for good.
    So since the Dash Diet is based on health principles, it promotes losing weight slower and therefore keeping the weight off. You will inevitably feel a bit of frustration at first as you are used to losing weight quickly, but will find that the success continues on. This is the way that your body was intended to lose weight and you will enjoy the long term view of this as well.

- It was created by medical professionals and not just some "expert" trying to make money:

Another key point to recognize is that the Dash Diet was developed by doctors and medical professionals. This goes a long way rather than just the opinions or money makers that dwell within the weight loss industry. Far too many diets are there to make companies or individuals money, and they don't put your best interest at heart.

Rest assured that since the Dash Diet was developed by medical professionals to help patients with a specific health condition, that it is all factual and therefore helpful. You don't have to be worried about wear and tear on your body and can feel comfortable that what you are doing is actually good for you.

- The Dash Diet will be there in the long term:

    So many fads and trends out there are set up for short term, quick hitting success, and then the failure is inevitable. It's not easy to explain that slower weight loss is better, but the longevity of the weight loss and the ability to keep that weight loss going is fundamentally important.

    The fads and trends will pass and change and therefore never be there to help you through the long term journey of weight loss. The Dash Diet is sound, proven, medically based, and will therefore be there to help you in the long term. You will enjoy weight loss until you get to your goal and if you follow the guidelines you will also see that the maintenance will be far easier as well.

How Can You Adapt This To Your Own Life?

So having the guidelines at your fingertips is an important first step. You now see what the Dash Diet is all about, you understand why it works, and you can utilize this information to move you forward. The hardest part of getting started though for so many people is how to figure out adapting these concepts to their own life. Seeing something in print is one thing but then getting it to work within your life is quite another.

This is where you need to put the principles into practice to ensure that you have the balance that you need to move forward. Simply reading through and comprehending what the Dash Diet is all about is great, but if you don't consider how this will apply to your own life then you will not get the progress that you are after. You need to consider what needs to happen to make this part of your life.

You Need An Action Plan To Really Make This Work

This is like setting goals for yourself and then never taking the time to write them down. This is like telling yourself that you are going to work out, but then never creating a fitness regimen to work off of. This is like saying that you need to eat healthier, but then never taking the time to shop for and prepare the foods that will help you to do so. Without the adaptation to your own life the Dash Diet will only be as effective as you allow it to be.

When you figure out how to adapt to the Dash Diet, this is where you are making the necessary lifestyle changes. You can't just will it to happen for you need to create the foundation that will ensure that it is successful. The Dash Diet is by far the most effective diet and vehicle out there to help you to reach long term weight loss. In order to allow it to be successful for you as an individual though, you need to determine what changes you will make to get it to work. Something that you are doing in your life isn't working for you right now, and it's time to focus on that and make the changes. To get the Dash Diet to work for you it's imperative to make the necessary changes and create the healthy lifestyle that will support these concepts — this is what will lead you to the success that you want!

How Can You Get This Proven Diet To Work For You?

It's not enough to just say that you want it to be successful, for you have to determine what will help to get you there. The Dash Diet is undoubtedly what will help you to lose the weight, but what sort of adaptations are you going to have to make in your life to make it work?
You will enjoy long term weight loss if you are willing and able to create a foundation set up to support you and to ensure that the concepts of the Dash Diet are followed properly. You need to create an action plan for success — and this is how you do it!

- Learn to budget your time to accommodate the activities needed to support this diet and lifestyle:

In order to make this weight loss plan work for you, it's necessary to budget your time appropriately. You might find that setting up the things you must to do as appointments works well as you are sure to keep them going that way. Set up appointments on your calendar for all of the things you must do, and then keep them as you would any other appointments.

Budget your time to accommodate activities such as exercising each day, shopping for the right foods, preparing and cooking these foods for the day and week, getting plenty of rest each night, and even set time aside for goal setting as necessary. This may sound silly, but if you allot the time and then dedicate your efforts to it then you are going to be far more likely to be successful.

- Think through what it will take for you to eat properly using these guidelines:

    You see the guidelines of what makes up good healthy eating using the Dash Diet, and now it's time to customize it a bit. So if you think of a given category for example lean proteins, you must consider what works well for you. Maybe you don't like fish for example, and so you focus your effort instead on eating poultry or alternative protein such as beans.

    If you have food allergies, food aversions, or special needs, then you need to figure out how to cater this program to you as an individual. The guidelines are there for you to use but within each category and eating plan, you must find what works out for your own balance. This is based on personal tastes and also mixing it up with variety to ensure that you stay with the program and remain dedicated and motivated.

Try a new food each week like a fruit or vegetable, incorporate new recipes, or try something totally different for breakfast. Customization and variety are going to be important ways of ensuring that you stick with this sort of eating plan.

- Be honest about the bad habits you need to get rid of and then do it once and for all:

There is something that has been keeping you from achieving success or making progress in the past. It's time to focus in on this and make this a thing of the past. Maybe you never stayed dedicated to a fitness regimen, and so now you must find a way to change that up and keep yourself motivated. Perhaps you gave up on your willpower and allowed in temptations at special occasions, and now it's time to put a stop to that.

Get rid of the bad habits that have been holding you back, and then you will be able to focus on what it takes to get to true long term success. To get the Dash Diet to work means that you get rid of anything that stands in the way of your progress. Perhaps it's as simple as not having time to make a healthy dinner each night and so you prepare your meals in advance to make it more convenient. Whatever it is, you must figure out the bad habits that hold you back and then switch it around so that you can enjoy the benefit of the Dash Diet.

Think through what it will take to get you to where you want to be, and then create healthy habits around this. You will enjoy the success when you set yourself up for it and that means adapting to this program in your everyday life — that's the only way to get it to really work for you!

Learning to Prepare For and Proactively Make This Diet Work In Your Lifestyle

Preparation is going to be the key to your success using this program. Though you may feel that this is an overwhelming task, if you keep at it this will become your norm before you realize it. You do have to determine what steps will be necessary for your own individual success, and then you must keep with them to make the progress that is required.
So how can this diet work within your life? What do you need to do to welcome it in? Well first and foremost you need to be sure that you set up and work through a healthy lifestyle to adapt to this sort of plan. A healthy lifestyle is the only way to do that and as you have seen by now that involves a lot of different factors at work altogether. Make the decision now to make changes and keep with them to make this diet an important part of your lifestyle.
Find Examples and Then Work Them Into Your Daily Life
Think through this one example at a time and then see how you can make the necessary and proactive changes. Start with something like salt—this is a substance that you should not be using on the Dash Diet so it's time to get rid of it. Excessive salt contributes to high blood pressure and can also be problematic to weight loss as well. So find salt substitutes and even alternatives such as fresh herbs that can give you all the flavor without any of the harmful elements.

That's just one example but you see that being proactive means that you take the power back as to what makes for a healthy lifestyle. This may mean figuring out what sort of low fat dairy you can tolerate and then focusing on it. This may mean trying new vegetables to add in the fiber which you have never considered before. There is always a way to make healthy provisions, and you need to be ready for them. By you being proactive and really working towards creating the right framework you can ensure that this diet is a success for you now and well into the future!

What Are The Best Proactive Measures and How Can You Institute Them?

Think of your life as it stands now and what it's going to take to make it healthy and welcoming to the principles of the Dash Diet. Much of this is going to come in the way of preparation and taking matters into your own hands. Don't ever give up and know that any amount of work that you put in is going to help you to overcome previous obstacles and set yourself up for success.

Being proactive, finding healthy alternatives, and carving time out of your day to take on the most helpful measures will all ensure that the Dash Diet is a realistic and successful measure in your life. Here's how to make it work and what you can do from a proactive point of view.

- Create a menu or eating plan at the beginning of every week:

  This should be a norm or a habit that you get into regardless of what you are doing at the time. The Dash Diet gives you the framework of what you can and should eat, but then the individual choices are up to you. In the interest of true preparation it's imperative that you set up menus or eating plans each and every week to keep you on track.

Think of what you have going on in a week and your daily schedules and then work your meals in. You want to work for balance amongst the foods that you are allowed and encouraged to eat. Initially creating a shopping list may seem like a lot of work, but some of the same items will begin to appear week after week. You also want to add in a bit of variety to keep your eating interesting and fun. Plan for every meal and snack and be sure that some of the food is transportable.

If you have the right healthy foods on hand you won't be tempted to cheat. Getting your shopping done in this way ensures that you have everything that you need and that you are always proactive and prepared for eating right and sticking with the Dash Diet program.

- Find recipes that will support eating in this way:

You will find some great sample recipes at the end of this book that can get you started. You will find that you want to find some of your own as you move forward. Variety is the key to staying engaged and to ensuring that you are successful with this diet. So begin to search for recipes and fun ways of eating the right foods.

This is a proactive measure that also works towards staying motivated. If you find a great recipe source or begin to become a bit creative on your own, then it will make cooking fun. You will never look at cooking as a chore, but rather a way of taking care of yourself and ensuring that you lovingly prepare the right meals.

- Make the time for the things that you need to truly take care of yourself:

Part of taking care of yourself involves making time to do the things you must do. To reiterate that means making time for exercise, for getting plenty of rest each night, and of course for eating healthy. That means that you make the time to eat smaller meals more frequently throughout the day.

This also means that you make the time to shop for, prepare, cook, and package up the healthy meals and snacks that you will eat all day long. This means that you have the ingredients on hand and put time aside to get it altogether. This can only be successful if you make time to take care of yourself in this manner. If you don't dedicate the time to search for recipes or to get fresh ingredients, then you won't be prepared and may fall into old bad habits.

Getting Rid Of The Wrong Foods and The Bad Habits

There comes a time when you need to make changes that are meaningful in your life. Sure in previous weight loss attempts you have likely limited yourself and focused on healthy eating, but probably for a limited time. In order to get the Dash Diet to work for you, then it's not about making limited time changes. This is about creating a lifestyle that works and supports you in losing weight and getting healthier.

The Dash Diet is focused on what makes for good, healthy, and proper eating. You see by now what makes for the right foods in the perfect blend. This will lead you not only to long lasting weight loss, but also better health as well. So you know what you need to focus on in terms of the right foods, but there's more to it than that.

What about the wrong foods? How do bad habits factor into this? The truth is that in order to let the good and proper nutrition of the Dash Diet work and really take place in our lives, we must first start by getting rid of the wrong things. This will only be as effective as the parameters that you set up around it. In order to make the good take effect, you must first usher out the bad.

Getting Rid of the Things That Are Holding You Back
This is about changing your lifestyle, but also your habits. This is about trying to avoid the "cheat" and getting rid of the excuses or justifications. If you know the food is bad for you, then avoid it. If you aren't sure then here is the list so that it's all clear. If you know that you need to change something that isn't working in your life, then now is the time to do so.

You must abandon once and for all the things that are holding you back, and seeing that list here will help you to move forward in the most productive manner possible. So here are the foods and habits that have likely caused you problems in the past and what you need to avoid and get away from in order to let the Dash Diet be effective and successful for you.

The List of Things to Avoid and Get Away From For Good

You know what the RIGHT things are to do and to eat, and now it's time to look at and fully understand what the WRONG things are. Here we look at a comprehensive list of which foods and habits have been keeping you from progress, and which must go away to make the Dash Diet take full effect.

- No more red meat:

    Sure you may enjoy it, but red meat is loaded with all of the wrong things. While it is a source of protein, it is also a fatty type at that. You will find plenty of other sources of protein that don't introduce so much fat and so many unwanted calories.
    If you think about why the Dash Diet was started it was to help relieve hypertension, and so it makes sense that red meat is off limits for this condition. So to make the Dash Diet work and be truly effective, you need to avoid red meat and know that a healthier and lower fat source of protein awaits you.
- No more salt:

This may sound like a tough one, but it's much easier than you might think. Sure there is a certain element of salt present in some foods, but that's not what we're referring to. We're talking about table salt that is added in preparation, in cooking, or even after the food is presented to you and ready to eat. This extra salt of course adds to the possibility of hypertension and can also lead to weight gain.

You retain a lot of water when you use excess salt and therefore you want to get this out of your diet. You can find some great salt substitutes or turn to other herbs or spices to offer flavor without the added sodium. Get rid of the salt and see some results from this almost immediately.

- No more processed or fried foods:

The processed or fried foods that you have eaten out of either temptation or convenience are holding you back! They are loaded with unwanted fat, calories, and excessive sodium and additives. They will never help your efforts and will only ever hurt your ability to lose weight.

Stop allowing yourself to eat these as you get no nutritional value out of them and therefore they must be avoided to allow the Dash Diet to really work for you.

- No more high fat dairy products:

There's a reason that the Dash Diet stipulates low fat dairy products—because the high fat versions offer you nothing that you need. If you turn to low fat cottage cheese, yogurt, and skim milk you get all of the nutrients and benefits of dairy products, but none of the fat.

Higher fat dairy products may taste better to you, but you will get used to the lower fat versions in no time. There's no reason to opt for a fuller fat dairy product, and every reason to avoid this group of foods.

- No more white sugar or flour, nor starchy foods:

This is one of the core foundations of the Dash Diet because as we know too much sugar is never a good thing. Neither is too much flour or starch for that matter. If you are going to eat carbohydrates then it's imperative to turn to whole grain versions that are loaded with fiber.

White sugar and flour and all such starchy foods are going to help you to feel full quickly and therefore cause your insulin to rise. About an hour later you will feel hungry and eat whatever you can find, and so the cycle continues. These simple carbohydrates will only hurt your weight loss effort with this cycle and they introduce all sorts of ingredients that will work against your weight loss efforts.

- No more unnecessary or unhealthy additives or preservatives:

Here's a great rule of thumb to always remember — if you can't pronounce it or don't really know or understand what it is, then don't eat it. There are far too many foods out there that are simply made up of additives and preservatives, and this ends up becoming toxins in the body.

The Dash Diet promotes clean, whole, and healthy eating, and the unnecessary additives and preservatives are simply holding you back. They will never give you anything that you need, so avoid them!

- Stop eating on the run:

Sure we're all busy and have hectic schedules, but eating on the run is never good for you. This leads to convenience based eating and that means that you turn to whatever sort of food choices are before you—and they are usually not good ones.

Take the time to prepare and cook healthy meals and snacks that you can take with you wherever you go. Then you have everything you need to make the right food choices. Take the time to sit down and eat whenever you can as this aids digestion and ensures that you eat the right portions in the appropriate way.

- No more skipping meals and then binging:

The extreme calorie counting, the deprivation, the starvation—all of this contributed to the weight loss and then weight gain cycle in the past. Never again! No more skipping meals or going to extremes when it comes to losing weight the right way.

You will only binge the next time you eat and this creates a very unhealthy cycle. You need to be sure to eat the right portions all day long. No more skipping meals, no more binging, and no more extremes when it comes to the way in which you eat. It's time to take care of yourself and that starts with what you eat and HOW you eat as well.

Making Changes For True and Long Lasting Weight Loss

The Dash Diet is going to take you to where you want to go, but you have to be willing to make the changes required to get there. This is going to lead you to long term and lasting weight loss, but you have to allow yourself to get there. Change is good, it's nothing to be feared, and it's going to mean everything in terms of your ability to succeed.

You've seen what is needed in terms of the right things to eat and the best way to create a healthy lifestyle. You understand the right foods to eat and how to eat them. You even know what it will take to get rid of the bad habits and which foods are off limits. The guidelines are all here for the taking, but now it's important to make the changes to get you there.

Different Kinds of Changes That Are Critical To Success

These changes have very little to do with diet specifically, but rather a willingness to get yourself into the right frame of mind and make it all happen for yourself. These changes come with a realization that you are in control, that you have the power and that the time to move forward with your life comes now. These changes are what will help to make this time truly different and ensure that this really IS long lasting weight loss. This is life changing!

To fully understand these changes you are going to have to dig deep. To really get to the brink of success you need to start with a personal transformation. You know and understand what makes for a solid weight loss platform now. Here are the personal and life changes that will really help you to discover your best success, in this area and beyond.

- The change starts from within you:

Know this — the ability and willingness to change and to want to change comes from within you! This can't come from anybody else, it can't work through anybody else, and it must be kept up from you and you alone. If you are trying to do this for somebody or something else then you will not be successful.

It is only when you discover that you have the ability to change and now you have to put forth the effort. You have to make the change happen and remain in control of this process at all times — it all starts and finishes from within you!

- This successful diet is only as good as the effort that you put forth:

   You are in control of your destiny here and that means that you have to put forth the effort. You can read up on this and comprehend this as much as you want, but what are you going to do to LIVE it? This is different for everyone and therefore the effort must come from you as a whole.
   Figure out your starting point, know your bad habits or temptations, be aware of what has held you back in the past and then be willing to break through these barriers. Understand that this successful program will only be successful for you if you allow it to be — and that means that some serious effort in all aspects of this program must come from you at the beginning and every step of the way.

- Understanding why you have failed in the past is pivotal to your success:

Learn from past mistakes and turn these into productive lessons from which to make change off of. If you slacked off on exercise in the past, then know that this is a weak spot for you and be sure that it doesn't hold you back this time. If you are aware that healthy eating is hard at certain times then set yourself up for success.

The changes that you make must be all around and versatile at that. You must be sure that you change the way that you live on a daily basis, but it's more than that. You also have to work through and change the previous patterns, habits, and behaviors that held you back previously. Though you may not want to think that the problems came from you specifically, learning from past failed attempts can only help you to be better this time around.

- Creating a healthy lifestyle with the right habits is what it's all about:

Change comes from the foods that we eat but also the way in which we eat them. Change comes from exercising, and also from getting a good night of sleep. Change comes from truly taking care of ourselves. So the Dash Diet is one major component of that, but the lifestyle that surrounds it will either support it or reject it in practice.

To be successful you need to lifestyle and the healthy habits to make this all work together. You will only be successful with the Dash Diet if you have a foundation and lifestyle that helps to support it. Without that your attempts will fall short and this will be like everything else. You need to make changes to help support what the Dash Diet can provide.

A healthy lifestyle is important for weight loss, but also for improved health. You are going to see by making all of these necessary changes just how much better you feel. Weight loss will undoubtedly be a major part of this, but so too will your ability to really enjoy being a whole new you.

This is where you improve your QUALITY of life and start enjoying all that lies ahead of you. This is where change helps you to transform yourself and make your weight loss journey a truly successful one. It's time to welcome a whole new you!

Staying Focused and Committed To a Program That Really Works In Your Future

The Dash Diet is going to work for you. The parameters of this diet plan are going to set you up for success. This is a program that you can e successful with. The power to do all of this and to make it all work comes from within you. So it's time to get in touch with those elements that will lead you to true and lasting weight loss success. Now it's time to really get started! First and foremost you need to remain focused and strong. That means overcoming previous hurdles and getting in touch with what worked against you in the past. That means that you figure out what held you back even with the worst diet program and then turn that into a positive energy for yourself. You can do this but you must be in touch with who you are and what you are all about.

Getting In Touch With What Makes You Do Well and What Causes You To Lose Focus

Everybody has had success and failure — in weight loss and well beyond, and now it's time to figure out how and why it occurred! Though you may feel as though you simply failed because of a faulty diet, more than likely there is something that you can get in touch with inside yourself to reveal how you can be better. Staying focused and committed is ultimately about doing much needed soul searching.

It's about confidence, strength, commitment, perseverance, and understanding yourself as a person. Once you can do that you will enjoy success not only within your ability to lose the weight and keep it off, but also within your life as a whole. Take a look inside yourself and determine what will help your level of commitment and then use this to power you forward. This is a great exercise that can really help, and here's how to remain focused at all times.

- Work through past hurdles and obstacles and know how to overcome them:

    Figure out what has caused you to fail, both in weight loss and overall, and then use that as a strength to your advantage. Figure out what sort of hurdles or obstacles are common or even present patterns for you and then figure out what it will take to get through them.

    These can be as simple as food temptations, a trend towards being lazy at certain times of day or year, or giving into a lack of willpower and just going crazy with the eating that you do. Whatever it is, you get in touch with those obstacles and then figure out how to overcome them. This is about remaining strong in the face of adversity and knowing that YOU truly have the power to make it through even the most challenging of circumstance.

- Go into this with a proactive approach and be ready for anything:

Know that you are going to have bad days. Recognize that you are going to fall off track sometimes. Be realistic about your approach and your journey and never give up, no matter what may come your way. Ultimately be proactive and be ready to welcome challenges and recognize that they are part of the journey.

If it wasn't hard then everybody would be successful. Anything worth working for is going to present its own challenges and it's up to you to overcome them. So if you can go in with a knowledge that the going may get tough and the proactive approach that you can handle it no matter what, you are going to get a lot further. Then you are prepared for anything and can really work through the challenges when they come at you without any surprises.

- Determine what will help your level of commitment as well as focus and then engage it every moment that you can:

Something has caused you to falter in the past and now you need to turn that negative into a positive. If you have struggled with focus in any area of your life, it's time to figure out exactly why that is. If you have had issues with focus or devotion or just had commitment issues overall, it's time to figure out a way to overcome that.

Perhaps you feel frustrated or you're just not happy with yourself. Maybe you feel beat down from previous weight loss attempts or don't give yourself the credit that you deserve. Maybe you have even been put down by others and therefore don't have the necessary self esteem to remain committed to anything.

This is where the soul searching becomes a must because if you have issues with focus and commitment, that is more than likely due to something. Some factor is present in your life that has taken this ability from you, and now it's time to put it to rest.

Don't give the negative factors power in your life but rather figure out how to move forward with a positive and strong viewpoint and make this all work for yourself. If you will it to and get in touch with what has held you back in the past, then you are going to love how great things work out this time. You truly have this power, but you have to get in touch with it and then use it moving forward.

- Find the inner strength within you to help you to stick with the program and work to the success that you so richly deserve:

You are much stronger than you give yourself credit for. Embrace that inner strength, unleash tat confidence, and use all of these skills and powers to help you to move forward. You now have the framework of the Dash Diet to help you to successfully lose the weight, but the power to actually make it happen comes from within you.
The reality is that you do have the strength, you do possess the skills and the focus and the determination and the confidence to know that you are worth it. You must believe this in order to make it work for you, and when you do then you are embracing your own strength. It really can be a powerful and beautiful thing, but first you must ensure that it is willed to happen.

If you don't feel confident and strong, then the Dash Diet will only take you so far. That inner strength will affect every action that you take and ensure that you really work towards long term success. You have to feel and believe that you are worth it before you begin the journey.

You have the program that will lead you to long term success and now it's up to you to put it to work using your power that you possess within you to make it happen. These are concepts that will lead you to long term success and help you to feel more valuable as a person — and you will get to enjoy the journey and life in general much more along the way!

Conclusion

There's a reason that the Dash Diet is so successful and why it has helped patients for years, not only to lower their blood pressure but also to lose weight. You are going to love how well this can work for you but you have to give it the platform for which to work through. You have to get yourself ready for what will ultimately be your greatest success in your life, but the journey begins with you.

As you have seen, the Dash Diet works because it works off of simple but highly effective health principles as the foundation. You will get to enjoy eating, but in the right way. You need a healthy lifestyle to set the platform and then it's about eliminating sugar, getting rid of the wrong carbohydrates, and turning away from the wrong foods and substances such as excess salt. These are solid concepts that you should already be using, and now it's up to you to put them to work in your life.

It's about what you eat and how you eat it, but it's also about ensuring that you exercise. It's about getting plenty of rest and just truly learning to take care of yourself for that will always be instrumental to your success in such a program. Though you may be sure that you have tried everything in the past, this time will be different because you are working through a well established, healthy, and proven weight loss program that will give you great results.

You are going to feel better, you are going to get healthier, and you are going to lose the weight slower but keep it off for good. This is the way that weight loss was intended to be and this journey will work so long as you stick with the program and really work to overcome previous obstacles. This is going to be as successful as you allow it to be, and that means that you put forth the effort needed to keep the weight off.

This is the right program and the right approach and if you embrace it and really make it work in your life, then you are going to absolutely love how you feel. There are great things ahead for you and if you maintain a confidence and willingness to make it all work in your life then your life will be richer for it. This is how you take off the weight and keep it off for good — this is how you become the person that you want to be and enjoy the life that you so richly deserve!

"Each patient carries his own doctor inside him."
— Norman Cousins, Anatomy Of An Illness

UPDATED ENHANCED EDITION! ADDITIONAL CHAPTERS ADDED!

Bonus Chapter: "DETOX"

Detoxifying is a Continuous Process!
Embrace this and Make it a Habit!

If you are trying to lose weight, cleanse your system or just wanting to be healthier, then detoxifying your body is what you need to do. This purifying process will make you feel so much better physically as well as mentally. You do not necessarily have to do a fast 3-day or 7-day detox, but, if that is what you want to try then go for it. Once you detox your body for the first time you will want to make this a continuing process for the rest of your life. Think about it, you do not have to take pills everyday or fast all the time or do strenuous exercise to purge and cleanse your system from unhealthy waste that is stored up in your body. You would be surprised at what is stored in your body from all the processed, fatty and junk food we consume as well as meat and dairy.

Your kidneys and liver can detoxify as well, but they too must be healthy. How can a weak liver and bad kidneys help you stay strong and in good health? By eating raw fruits and vegetables as well as nuts you are helping yourself become a well person. When your food is not constantly heated and cooked the vitamin and mineral content stay intact, which means the enzymes that help with digestion are able to do their job. Organic and all natural fruits and vegetables are the best to consume because they have no pesticides. If you are allergic to nuts then eat seeds (sunflower, pumpkin, chia). When you are going through your detox period why not try alternative products like dairy free or gluten free foods such as rice milk instead of cow's milk. Did you know that rice milk is easier to digest than cow's milk?

This is a non-conventional detox program and you can try to start one step at a time, and there is no rush, progress at your own pace. You can achieve everything even if you make small changes and adjustments, and there is no need for drastic changes.

A journey of a thousand miles begins with a single step.
   Lao-tzu, The Way of Lao-tzu

For example, if you eat a hamburger and French fries with a soda for lunch every day, then next time skip the fries or replace fries with a few carrots, and that will be the first step towards detoxification. Likewise, replace a soda with a bottle of water. Even better, instead of a hamburger replace it with chicken or turkey or may be a fish sandwich. That is some progress. We call this a progressive detoxification scheme (program)!

We can always introduce a few items to detoxify, like Ginger tea, or may be mint tea, or how about Yogic breathing to help the digestion for natural detoxification?
(details in recipe section).
Replace some of the bad foods with good foods, one at a time, and improve upon your healthy eating habits, which is the best detoxification as that will last a life time.

Replace some of the low glycemic foods with high fiber, low glycemic items, and avoid some of the bad fats, higher calorie foods, and replace some of the junk food with super foods, like avocado, berries, coconut, etc. (refer to the list of bad foods vs good food at the end of this chapter) (Also refer to the glycemic index chart provided in the later part of this chapter, as that will help you decide to choose low glycemic indexed foods).

Detoxification is nothing more than lowering the process workload of your body (especially liver and kidney). Give your body a break, and you will eventually feel so much better and happier, physically and emotionally. Because emotionally you will know you are on the right track to wellness and physically your body will genuinely feel well. You will thank us for that (your body will thank you for that break)!

Please refer to this Govt. resource for further education on Dash Diet. You should also consult your Doctor before making any changes in your lifestyle and diet.

http://www.nhlbi.nih.gov/health/public/heart/hbp/dash/how_make_dash.html

Favorable Items (add to your diet and prefer to eat)

(YES LIST)

Water
High Fiber
Grains
Fruits
Vegetables
Lean Meat
Fish
Fat free or Low Fat Dairy (limited qty)
Good Fats and Oils (limited)
Nuts, Seeds, and Legumes

Eat more: Potassium and Magnesium Rich Foods:

Sweet Potatoes
Swiss Chard
Apples
Celery
Broccoli
Collard Greens
Cantaloupes
White Beans
Tomatoes
Beet Greens
Dark Leafy Greens (Spinach)
Baked Red Potatoes (With Skin)
Green Beans
Clams
Prunes
Carrots
Apricots
Acorn Squash
Winter Squash
Low Fat Milk
Oranges
Sunflower Seeds
Beans
Soybeans
Yogurt (Skim/Non-Fat)

Fish (Salmon)
Avocados
Mushrooms
Bananas

Favorable Items (add to your diet and should prefer to eat)

(YES LIST)

Foods Highest in Antioxidants Contents

Rank	Food	Serving Size	Total C s
1	Small Red Bean	1/2 cup dried beans	13727
2	Wild blueberry	1 cup	13427
3	Red kidney bean	1/2 cup dried beans	13259
4	Pinto bean	1/2 cup	11864
5	Blueberry	1 cup cultivated berries	9019
6	Cranberry	1 cup whole berries	8983
7	Artichoke hearts	1 cup cooked	7904
8	Blackberry	1 cup	7701
9	Prune	1/2 cup	7291
10	Raspberry	1 cup	6058
11	Strawberry	1 cup	5938
12	Red Delicious apple	1	5900
13	Granny Smith	1	5381
14	Pecan	1 ounce	5095
15	Sweet cherry	1 cup	4873
16	Black plum	1	4844
17	Russet potato	1 cooked	4649
18	Black bean	1/2 cup dried beans	4181
19	Plum	1	4118
20	Gala apple	1	3903

Remove, Reduce These Items From Your Diet

(NO LIST)

Refined Carbs (FAST CARBS): instantly spike your blood sugar and triggers your body's insulin response. Ultimately this raises your blood pressure.
TOP Worst Fast Carb Foods:
White Bread (Toast/Bagel/Muffins, etc.)
Energy Drinks/Sodas/Sweetened Beverages
Pancakes/Waffles etc.
Jellies/Jams/Fruit Pies, etc.
Crackers
Chips
Boxed Cereals
White Flour Tortillas
White Potatoes: Mashed/French Fries etc.
White Rice

White Flour Pasta
Junk Food
Sodas, Soft drinks
Fried Food
Highly Processes Meats
Starchy, High - Glycemic Foods
REFINED Vegetable Oils (Please trust me)
Margarine
Foods Containing Hydrogenated (or partially hydrogenated) Oils
Ketchup
Excess Alcohol
Bad Fats
Sugars
Excess Caffeine
Excess Salt
Excess Fatty Foods (cut all bad fats)
Excess High Calories (you consume daily)

You know your body, personality and habits and you are the one who should be deciding about what detox plan works for you and in fact you should be able to create your own detox plan. You can always start small and then see how you feel and gradually try the next level of detoxification of the same item or another.

Detox: one item a day!
Detox at your own pace!
Detoxifying is a Continuous Process!

Adopt this and Make it a Habit!

Try these healing spices and herbs to flavor your foods

<u>Many herbs and spices are known to help lower blood pressure:</u>

- Cayenne pepper (cayenne pepper is a powerful vasodilator, and may help expand blood vessels and ultimately help improve blood flow)

- Coconut water (full of nutrients, specially potassium, may help lower blood pressure levels)

- Raw Cacao (flavonoids and other anti-inflammatory nutrients in raw cacao may help deal the stress which is one of big cause of blood pressure problem)

- Turmeric (curcumin).(super food turmeric might help fight inflammation in the whole body, ultimately helping improve cardiovascular function and maintenance of healthy blood flow.)

- Basil (It might help lower your blood pressure)

- Ginger root: (might help fight inflammation in the whole body, ultimately helping improve cardiovascular function and maintenance of healthy blood flow)

- Lavender: (Lavender's leaves can be used in the same as you use rosemary. This relaxation herb may help lower your blood pressure)

- Cardamom (anti-oxidant, anti-inflammatory)

- Celery Seeds (anti-oxidant, anti-inflammatory)

- Hawthorn: (Hawthorn had been used in China for centuries to help lower high blood pressure)

- Red Hot Chili Pepper (Hot Chili peppers contain capsaicin that is known to increase metabolism and can help in weight loss. The weight loss can ultimately help lower blood pressure)

- Nutmeg: (Contains anti-inflammatory compounds, and may also help you stay calm by helping regulating mood swings, ultimately lower blood pressure)

- Rosemary: (Rosemary's anti- inflammation properties may help lower blood pressure)

- Cloves: (Good anti-inflammatory)

- Capers: (Antioxidants, vitamins, analgesic, anti-inflammatory)

- Black Pepper: (Good anti-inflammatory)

- Cayenne Pepper: (concentrated with minerals, vitamins and certain phytochemicals/nutrients, popular for anti-diabetic properties)

- Carom Seeds (Ajwain) (ajowan seeds are rich in fiber, minerals, vitamins, and anti-oxidants)

- Coriander Seeds (full of anti-oxidants, and excellent source of minerals like iron, copper, calcium, potassium, manganese, zincand magnesium)

- Fennel Seed: (contains numerous flavonoid anti-oxidants like kaempferol and quercetin. act as powerful anti-oxidants by removing harmful free radicals)

- Horseradish: (dietary fiber, vitamins, minerals, anti-oxidants, diuretic, have nerve soothing effects, anti-inflammatory)

- Mustard Seeds: (rich in phyto-nutrients, minerals, vitamins and anti-oxidants, regulating body metabolism)

- Tamarind: (certain health benefiting essential volatile chemical compounds, minerals, vitamins and dietary fiber.)

- Onion: (Antiseptic, may helps reduce high blood pressure, alleviates symptoms of asthma and colds)

- Sichuan Peppercorns: (source of vitamins such as vitamin A, carotenes, pyridoxine, and thiamin and minerals - manganese, potassium , copper, iron, phosphorous, selenium and zinc.)

- Lemon Peel: (Good source of minerals and vitamin C, a good cleaning agent, Alleviates congestion)

- Orange Peel: Good source of minerals and vitamin C, a good cleaning agent, Alleviates congestion)

- Peppermint: (anti-inflammatory, antioxidant, digestive aide)

The following pages contains a chapter from our other book and this is just to demonstrate to you a detox plan, a plan about detoxifying your body by eliminating carbs and sugar from your diet. We thought this might help you understand the detoxification process.

BONUS CHAPTER! SAMPLE DETOX PLAN

A Sugar Detox Diet

"Just because you're not sick doesn't mean you're healthy"
~Author Unknown

By now, you should have a fairly good idea of why sugar can and should be cut from the diet. You can get plenty of all natural energy (glucose) without eating anything that has been processed. Sugar triggers drug like activities in the brain, prevents your "satiety" factor to tell you that you are overdoing it and/or are "full", and keeps you on a roller coaster in which you "crash" as insulin puts sugar into storage and then makes you hungry again very soon afterward.

Clearly, there is so much wrong with sugar that it becomes a mystery as to why we haven't made a point of cutting it out of our diets sooner. However, there is the commercial factor to consider. A bit later on we are going to look at some conspiracy theory-like issues connected to sugar in processed foods, and even why women might be more prone to sugar addiction than some men.

For now, we just need to remember that sugar is no one's friend. In fact, the human body has been designed to burn fat rather than sugar as a form of energy, and yet fat tends to have a much worse reputation than sugar or simple carbs. Why? It can be linked to those conspiracy theories we'll discuss a bit later, but it also has to do with simple misunderstandings and misinformation. Because we don't want to "be fat", many of us assume we shouldn't eat it. This is, actually, backwards thinking!

For instance, we've almost all heard about diets such as the globally famous Atkins and South Beach diets. These are two ways of eating that require you to cut carbs to extreme levels and emphasize healthy fats

Diets of this kind might limit specific food groups - such as vegetables that are on the starchy side, and even ask that you forgo things like bread, grain, and potatoes during a one or two week period. Again, this is to help the body detox, but some of these plans are a bit off the mark.

For instance, they allow people to eat dangerously high amounts of "saturated" fat, and that is never advisable as it can clog arteries and create unhealthy amounts of cholesterol in the blood stream. It is only with a balanced approach to eating that you can cut your sugar habits and remain in the peak of health.

While it is entirely true that the body uses fat far more efficiently than it does sugar (when it is for creating energy it normally gives twice the amount of energy that sugar carbs will), it still has to be a "safer" fat.

This usually means a monounsaturated variety, with only limited amounts of polyunsaturated and saturated allowed. For example, avocados and nuts are often said to be fattening because they do have a high amount of it, but they both contain only small amounts of saturated fat. They are nutrient dense foods with a lot to offer and are much better for you than some whole wheat bread or a cup of artificially sweetened yogurt.

Confusing right? Let's take a few moments more to assess this issue.

Optimal Energy

Consider that human evolution occurred over a period of time during which hunter/gatherers became farmers. Because food was always an issue for the hunter and gatherer, their bodies began to evolve storage systems for any calories that they did not use. When the body did need energy, it could burn up that little bit of fat as needed. They could also exist off of a huge variety of different foods - which is rare in the animal kingdom.

For example, one day a human being might ingest a huge quantity of meat from a freshly killed animal, but the next day they might be able to forage only a huge number of berries and leaves. The human body is capable of synthesizing most of what it needs from a diet as diverse as this, and this is a major benefit for modern eaters too.

Modern humans don't need to store any substantial amounts of fat because we are rarely living as hunter/gatherers any longer. Instead, we should be eating fat as a major energy source because it is put to use in the body almost as soon as it is eaten. It is not processed in the same ways that carbs are, and modern people have made the grievous error of conditioning their bodies to burn sugar rather than relying on fat.

Smarter diets, similar to those we just mentioned above are actually designed to start reprogramming the body to use fat for energy, but some grossly overlook the hazards of eating too much saturated fat and cholesterol, and cutting out the nutrients and fiber from fruits and vegetables. The sugar detox approach is less rigid and encourages you to eat a diet that is natural, balanced, and which features complex carbs and fiber.

A Good Example

To better understand an optimal diet, it helps to think of the body like a car that needs diesel fuel to run, but for which there is only rocket fuel available. Now, that little car can realistically burn up the rocket fuel to operate, but it would eventually damage a lot of the different parts and systems doing so.

Your body is being damaged by every spoonful of sugar or simple carb that you eat because it is creating a type of fuel that, while useable, is not ideally suited as a primary source of energy.

Sugars and simple carbs will burn up fast and create "wasted" energy that has to be put somewhere, and it is turned into…you guessed it…fat.

Just stop to consider what our bodies store - they store fat. This is because it is the ideal material for the body to use as energy. If sugar was the ideal fuel, the body would be designed to store a lot of sugar, but it doesn't.

This means that a sugar detox diet is going to help you to convert your body back into a fat burning system rather than one that is being constantly conditioned to deal with sugar. However, it is not all that easy to do this.

It requires you to begin retraining yourself, and this often means you will have to re-learn how to eat. Earlier in this book we mentioned the typical breakfast of OJ and a bagel. The first three to five days that you don't eat this, it is going to feel very odd. That big glass of orange sweetness and that huge load of carbs from the bagel are going to be sorely missed.

However, by the fifth to seventh day of burning up fat for energy, you are going to feel a bit sick thinking about guzzling a glass of sugary juice. Instead, you will actually crave the egg white omelet full of spinach and mushrooms or the handful of almonds and the cup of plain Greek yogurt. Why? You will have cured yourself of the sugar habit/addiction and started feeling all of the amazing benefits.

A Day in the Life

So, what exactly does a day on a sugar detox diet look like? Well, a good "starter" menu would look like this:

- Breakfast:
    - 1/2 cup plain oatmeal (not instant)
    - 1 tbsp flax seed
    - 3 egg whites

- Snack:
    - 1 tbsp unsweetened, all natural peanut butter
    - 1 apple
- Lunch:
    - 4 oz grilled chicken breast
    - 2 cups mixed salad vegetables - include greens, peppers, and cucumbers
    - Splash of balsamic vinegar as dressing
    - 1/2 sweet potato
- Snack
    - 1 cup raw veggies
    - 4 tbsp homemade hummus
- Dinner:
    - 4 oz broiled salmon
    - 1 cup green vegetables (raw or cooked)
    - 2 cups mixed salad veggies - including greens
    - Splash of balsamic to dress salad
    - 1/2 sweet potato

- Late night snack:

    o 1/4 (around 15) almonds

- At least 8 glasses of water (from 6-8 ounces each) and some green tea for energy

You can see that there are plenty of carbs on this plan, it is simply that they come in the form of a fresh vegetables, fruits, fats, and protein.

In fact, this single day shows the sort of "pyramid" that most people will begin to follow as they shift from a heavily laden carbohydrate-rich diet to one that is meant to burn fat for energy and eliminate cravings for sugar.

The pyramid we describe would feature healthy fats as the largest portion of the diet, lean proteins as the next level, non-starchy vegetables after that, a small amount of allowable carbs (complex from fruit or some grains), and little to no sugar.

What would happen when you started eating like that? That is what we now consider…

What to Expect

First of all, the diet is called a "detox" for very obvious reasons - you are detoxifying the body. And just like all other types of detox, you will face some serious challenges. These include:

- Headache

- Irritability (some people experience substantial and relatively "wild" irritability)

- Cravings

- Body aches

- Congestion

- Sluggishness and low energy

- Hazy thinking

- High emotional states

- Skin changes (remember, your body is adjusting and releasing toxins which can cause rashes, acne, and irritation)

- Dizziness

- Interest in foods that supply simple carbs (for example, you may always be a cookie and cake eater and yet find yourself suddenly craving a lot of potatoes and bread - this is a form of addiction transference and is a sign that your body already knows where to get a sugar fix if needed).

- Dehydration

- Cold and flu like symptoms

- Bloating or gas

- Body odor and bad breath

- Disrupted sleep patterns

- Strange thoughts

The good news is that a lot of people who do this diet will often agree that by the fourth or fifth day of remaining free of sugar they are feeling much stronger. After two weeks a lot of people are confident that they have this particular issue "kicked", and after three weeks, most people feel so much better that they don't even go for the "celebratory" sugar options.
In other words, of all of the negatives listed above, few will remain by day four or five. So, ask yourself if optimal health is worth enduring three to five days of problems? Yes…it is!

This chapter is from the book
#1 Best Selling Book:: ASIN: B00GUXOCNM

Weight Loss by Quitting Sugar and Carb - Learn How to Overcome Sugar Addiction - A Sugar Buster Super Detox Diet... by Shawn Chhabra, Milo E Newton **and Jacqueline Harrington (Nov 2, 2013)**

Glycemic Index

This is taken from http://www.whfoods.com and credit goes to Robert Crahyon, M.S.
Living a Healthy Life the Low Glycemic Way

A helpful way of looking at high and low GI carbohydrates is explained by Robert Crahyon, M.S., promoter of the "Paleolithic Diet." Crahyon divides carbohydrates into two groups:

- Paleocarbs. The carbohydrates that sustained early mankind, the hunter-gatherers: vegetables, fruits and possibly tubers. All these carbohydrates are rich in fiber, vitamins and minerals — plus, most have a low GI.

- Neocarbs. Carbohydrates that developed as a result of agriculture: grains, legumes and flour products, then eventually, processed grain products such as those made with white flour and sugar, which have a high GI.

The majority of the World's Healthiest Foods are paleocarbs. Most of these foods have a low GI and will nourish, satisfy and energize you, while helping keep your blood sugar levels on an even keel.

The wholesome members of the World's Healthiest Foods that do have a higher GI can also be enjoyed in moderation, eaten along with low GI foods to balance their potential effect on your blood sugar levels.

For example, for breakfast, you might want to have oatmeal. Choose thick, dehulled oat flakes to make your oatmeal (these have a lower GI than rolled oats or one-minute oats), then eat grapefruit (one of the lower GI fruits) with your oatmeal rather than a banana (a fruit with a higher GI), and toss a few nuts or seeds over the oatmeal (nuts and seeds tend to have extremely low GIs). Finally, sprinkle a little cinnamon over your oatmeal. Recent studies have found that compounds in cinnamon can stimulate our cells' insulin receptors, increasing the cells' ability to absorb and use glucose. In this way, you can reduce the GI of your oatmeal and enjoy a nourishing breakfast that will provide you with plenty of energy all morning.

Below are the approximate GI values of many popular foods:

Food Source	GI per Serving
Watermelon	103
Potato	93
Rice Cake	91
Pretzels	85
Cornflakes cereal	84
Jelly Beans	80
Donut	76
Waffles	76
White Rice	72
Bagel	72
Wheat Crackers	70
Whole Wheat Bread	69
Honey	58
Pita	57
Banana	56
Brown Rice	55
Oatmeal (instant)	49
Carrots	49

Grapes	46
Spaghetti	43
Apple	38
Beans and Lentils	35
Yogurt	35
Milk (low fat)	32
Milk (whole)	22
Nuts	20
Broccoli	10
Cabbage	10
Lettuce	10
Onions	10
Mushrooms	10
Peppers	10
Meats	0
Canned fish	0
Seafood	0
Poultry	0

UPDATED ENHANCED EDITION! ADDITIONAL CHAPTERS ADDED!

Few Recipes

Mediterranean Chicken and Red Potatoes

A delicious blend of flavors that is inspired by classic Mediterranean ideas, and that means that you will love every bite. The potatoes are in the perfect amount and it shows that you can have a classic favorite without any of the guilt. So good that you may make this a regular part of the meal rotation and enjoy just how delicious healthy cooking can really be.

Ingredients:
1 1/2 lbs. boneless skinless chicken breasts, cut into 1-inch cubes
1 lb. Yukon Gold potatoes, cut into 3/4-inch cubes
1 medium onion, coarsely chopped
1/2 cup reduced-fat Greek or olive oil vinaigrette
1/4 cup lemon juice
1 tsp dry oregano
1 tsp minced garlic
1/2 cup chopped tomato

Preparation:
Mix all ingredients except tomatoes in a large bowl. Place equal amounts onto 4 large squares of heavy-duty foil. Fold in top and sides of each to enclose filling, leaving room for air to circulate.
Grill over medium heat for about 25 to 30 minutes or until chicken is cooked through and red potatoes are soft. Carefully open packets and sprinkle equal amounts of tomato over each.
Note: Packets may also be baked at 400°F for 30 minutes instead of grilling.

Nutty Mahi-Mahi

What You Need:

4 Mahi - Mahi fillets (8 oz)
4 eggs
4 cups Whole Wheat (unsalted) bread crumbs
½ cup Pine nuts
½ cup sliced (bleached) almonds
2 tsp fresh lemon juice
4 to 8 leaves fresh mint leaves
4 tsp olive oil

What You need to Do:

1. In a blender (food processor), blend the nuts (pine nuts and almonds), with bread crumbs, eggs, lemon juice, mint leaves and olive oil.
2. Marinate the fish with this blended marinate and refrigerate for 2 hours.
3. Pre heat the oven to 375 to 400 degree F and bake the fish for about 20 minutes (until cooked well).
4. Enjoy hot and fresh!
5. You can also try with brown rice or quinoa.

Makes 4 Servings

Garlic Shrimp

Hot Level:
Ice Cold, **Mild**, Spicy, Flaming, Scorcher

Prep Time: 15 minutes
Cook Time: 6 minutes

What You'll Need:

- 3 cloves of minced garlic
- 1/3 cup olive oil

- ¼ cup tomato sauce
- 2 tablespoons red wine vinegar
- 2 tablespoons fresh basil
- 2 pounds of shrimp
- ¼ teaspoon cayenne pepper

What You'll Do:

1. Mix up the garlic and tomato sauce and vinegar and oil. Add in the   basil, and pepper.
2. Put in the shrimp and stir. Put in the refrigerator for about 45 minutes.
3. Grill for about 3 minutes or so on each side, then eat.

Grilled Shrimp

What You'll Need:

- 3 cloves of minced garlic
- - 1/3 cup olive oil
- - ¼ cup tomato sauce
- 2 tablespoons red wine vinegar
- - 2 tablespoons fresh basil
- 2 pounds of shrimp
- - ¼ teaspoon cayenne pepper

What You'll Do:

1. Mix up the garlic and tomato sauce and vinegar and oil. Add in the basil, and pepper.

2. Put in the shrimp and stir. Put in the refrigerator for about 45 minutes.
3. Grill for about 3 minutes or so on each side, then eat.

Curry Chicken

Ingredients:

4 PCS Chicken breast (boneless, skinless) (cut into bite size cubes)
1 medium (chopped) onion
4 minced garlic cloves
1 medium ginger rood (chopped)
1 Medium size tomatoes
1 small can of (UNSLATED) tomato sauce
2 tsp curry powder
1 tsp turmeric powder
2 tsp *Garam Masala* (from Indian Grocery Store or Trader Joe's)
½ tsp. cumin powder
1/4 tsp. hot chili powder
3 tbsp. olive oil
Sea salt and ground pepper to taste (less salt is better)

Procedure:

1. In a large skillet on medium-low heat, add olive oil, sauté chopped onions until soft (about 4 to 7 minutes). Add the chopped garlic, minced garlic, the all the spices and cook 2 minutes.
2. Add chopped tomatoes, and tomato sauce. Whisk thoroughly and begin to bring to a simmer.
3. Add the chicken pieces, cover for 15 minutes, or until chicken is done.
4. Enjoy hot and fresh!
5. You can also try with brown rice or quinoa.

   Makes 4 Servings

Ginger-Garlic Mahi-Mahi Fillets

What you need:

4 Mahi - Mahi fillets (8 oz)
1 Cup low fat yogurt
4 tsp balsamic vinegar
1 tsp fresh lemon juice
2 tsp grated fresh ginger root
2 clove crushed garlic
6 tsp olive oil
Black pepper to taste

What You need to Do:

1. In a big bowl, mix yogurt, lemon juice, balsamic vinegar, ginger, garlic and half of the olive oil (3tbsp). Season fish filets with black pepper. Put the mahi-mahi fillets in this bowl (rub the fish with the mixture of this marinate).
2. Cover the marinated fish in the bowl and put in the refrigerator for 1/2 to 1 hour.
3. Heat the rest of the olive oil (3tbsp) in a large skillet over medium heat. Remove fish from the bowl, and reserve yogurt-marinade. Fry fish for about 5 minutes (each side). Pour rest of the yogurt-marinade over the fish in the pan and heat over medium heat for 2-3 minutes
4. Enjoy hot and fresh!
5. You can also try with brown rice or quinoa.

   Makes 4 Servings

Garlic Lemon Zest Mahi-Mahi Fillets

What you need:

4 Mahi - Mahi fillets (8 oz)
4 tsp balsamic vinegar
2 tsp fresh Lemon Juice
1/4 cup grapefruit juice
2 tsp grated fresh Lemon Zest
1tsp Lemon salt
2 clove crushed garlic
6 tsp olive oil

What You need to Do:

1. In a big bowl, mix all the ingredients to make the marinate.
2. Put the mahi-mahi fillets in this bowl (rub the fish with the mixture of this marinate).
3. Cover the marinated fish in the bowl and put in the refrigerator for 3 to 4 hour.
6. Pre heat the oven to 375 to 400 degree F and bake the fish for about 20 minutes (until cooked well).
7. Enjoy hot and fresh!
4. You can also try with brown rice or quinoa.

   Makes 4 Servings

Grilled Ginger Chicken

Ingredients:

1 cup Orange juice
1 medium size piece of fresh ground ginger root
6 tsp olive oil
2 Freshly crushed garlic cloves
4 PCS Chicken breast (boneless, skinless)

Procedure:

1. Mix all the ingredients to make the marinate.
2. Marinate the chicken breast pieces and refrigerate for 2 hours.
8. Pre heat the oven to 400 degree F and bake the chicken pieces for about 25 to 30 minutes (until cooked well).
9. Enjoy hot and fresh!
5. You can also try with brown rice or quinoa.

Makes 4 Servings

Grilled Basil-Thyme-Ginger Chicken

Ingredients:

3 tsp. fresh Thyme, chopped
3 tsp. fresh Basil, chopped
1 cup Tomatoes with juice
1 medium size piece of fresh ground ginger root
6 tsp olive oil
4 PCS Chicken breast (boneless, skinless)

Procedure:

3. Mix all the ingredients to make the marinate.
4. Marinate the chicken breast pieces and refrigerate for 2 hours.
10. Pre heat the oven to 400 degree F and bake the chicken pieces for about 25 to 30 minutes (until cooked well).
11. Enjoy hot and fresh!
6. You can also try with brown rice or quinoa.

Makes 4 Servings

Main Dish: *The Perfect Hardboiled Egg*
What You'll Need:
- 1 tablespoon of salt
- 6 cups of water
- 8 eggs
- ¼ cup distilled white vinegar

What You'll Do:
1. Mix together the salt and water and vinegar in a big pot.
2. Add the eggs before the water begins to boil.
3. Bring it to a boil on high.
4. Reduce the heat to a low setting and cook for 14 minutes or so.

5. Remove and cool. Enjoy plain or with any other entrée or side.

Sides
Baked Kale Chips

What You'll Need:
- 1 bunch of kale
- 1 tablespoon olive oil

What You'll Do:

6. Preheat oven to 350 degrees F and line a non-insulated cookie sheet with parchment paper.
7. Remove the leaves from the stems and tear them into bite-sized pieces. Wash them carefully and dry.
8. Drizzle olive oil over top the kale.
9. Bake until the edges are brown, about 10-15 minutes.

Sides:
Sugar Snap Peas
What You'll Need:
- ½ pound sugar snap peas
- 1 tablespoon olive oil
- 1 tablespoon chopped shallots
- 1 teaspoon chopped thyme
- Kosher salt to taste (**NO SALT IS BETTER**!)

What You'll Do:
1. Preheat oven to 450 degrees F.
2. Spread the peas onto a baking sheet.
3. Brush them with the olive oil.
4. Add on the shallots, thyme, and salt on top of the peas.
5. Bake the peas for 6 to 10 minutes (until firm but not burnt).

Cool and enjoy.

Mojito Punch

What You'll Need:

- ½ cup lime juice
- ½ cup fresh mint leaves
- -1/2 stevia (sweetner)
- 4 ¼ cups   soda
- 4 cups crushed ice

What You'll Do:

1. Combine the lime juice, mint leaves, and sweetener together in a bowl or pitcher.
2. Take the mint leaves and lightly bruise them with a spoon.
3. Pour the   soda into the juice mixture and add the sweetener.
4. Mix in the crushed ice and serve cold.

Spiced Applesauce

What You'll Need:

- 15 apples, peeled, cored, diced
- 1 teaspoon ground cinnamon
- 1 cup water
- 1/2 teaspoon grated nutmeg
- 1 tablespoon lemon juice
- 1/2 teaspoon ground allspice
- -1/2 stevia (sweetner)
- 1/2 teaspoon ground black pepper

What You'll Do:

1. Mix apples, water, lemon juice, and *stevia* in a pot on medium heat. Add cinnamon, nutmeg, allspice, and pepper.
2. Simmer the mixture while stirring and cook for around 15 minutes.
3. Mash the apples until preferable consistency.
4. Remove the pot and cool the applesauce in the refrigerator. Take out and serve cold.

Smoothie

What You'll Need:

- ½ cup plain Greek yogurt
- ¼ cup frozen blueberries
- 1/3 cup unsweetened almond milk
- 1 cup loosely packed spinach
- 1 scoop vanilla protein powder
- 1/3 cup ice

What You'll Do:

1. Add ingredients, two at a time, and blend until smooth and creamy.
2. Add ice last and serve cold.

Tabbouleh

This Mediterranean favorite is so good for you, but you can make it even healthier. Using concepts and acceptable ingredients on the Dash Diet you can forever change this into an even better alternative. Eat it on its own as a side dish or appetizer or enjoy it as a salad for lunch or dinner. You will love the burst of flavors!

Serves 8
<u>Ingredients</u>
1 1/2 cups water
3/4 cup bulgur (cracked wheat), rinsed and drained
1 cup diced, seeded tomatoes
1 cup chopped parsley
1/2 cup chopped scallions or green onions
1 teaspoon dill weed
4 black olives, sliced
1/4 cup lemon juice
2 tablespoons extra-virgin olive oil
Freshly ground black pepper, to taste
<u>Preparation:</u>
In a small saucepan, bring the water to a boil. Remove from heat and add the bulgur. Cover and let stand until the bulgur is tender and the liquid is completely absorbed, about 15 to 20 minutes.
In a large bowl, add the bulgur and the remaining ingredients. Toss gently just until the ingredients are evenly distributed. Cover and refrigerate for 2 hours to allow the flavors to blend. Serve chilled.

Mediterranean Bean Dip

This is one of those snacks that you could just live on! You will love the flavors all coming together and enjoy this unique twist on a classic bean dip. Rather than purchasing an already made bean dip that is full of fat and sodium, this makes for a great twist that is right in line with eating on the Dash Diet.

Ingredients:
2 15-ounce cans, rinsed and drained, or 3 1/2 cups cooked garbanzo or navy beans
2/3 cup fat-free sour cream
2 tsp minced garlic
4 tbsp balsamic vinegar
1/4 cup chopped sun-dried tomatoes (not in oil)
1/4 cup finely chopped fresh or dried parsley
2 tbsp chopped Kalamata or ripe olives
Kalamata olives, as garnish
Assorted vegetables and crackers for serving

Preparation:
In the bowl of a food processor blend the beans, sour cream, garlic, and vinegar until smooth; stir in sundried tomatoes, parsley, and chopped olives.
Place the mix in a serving bowl and garnish with olives. Serve with assorted vegetables and crackers for dipping.
Dip can be made ahead of time and refrigerated overnight or for 2 to 3 hours to allow flavors to blend.

Sides:
Roasted Garlic

What You'll Need:

- One head of garlic, medium sized
- 2 tablespoons of olive oil

What You'll Do:
1. Preheat the oven to 250 degrees F.
2. Cut the top off the clove of garlic and put into a dish for baking.
3. Add olive oil on top and bake for 20 minutes.
4. Cool and then use hands to squeeze out the soft garlic.

Fruity Fruit Juice
What You'll Need:
- 1 Granny Smith apple
- 1 pear
- 1 pitted peach

What You'll Do:
6. Yet another simple, yet delicious recipe. All you have to do is juice and serve.

Best chilled

Veggie Juice

What You'll Need:
- 1 beet
- 4 carrots
- 1 cucumber
- 3 celery stalks

What You'll Do:
10. Probably the simplest recipe out there—juice and serve.
11. Tastes great chilled or warm.

Drinks *Triple sec*
What You'll Need:
- 1 tomato
- 4 celery stalks
- 4 carrots

What You'll Do:

12. Juice and serve right away.
13. For a twist on this delicious drink, add a couple of your favorite spices and serve warm.

Crunchy Edamame

What You'll Need:

- 1 (12 ounce) package edamame or green soybeans (frozen and without shells)

 -1/2 spoon black peppers

- 1 tablespoon olive oil

What You'll Do:

1. Preheat oven to 400 degrees F.
2. Rinse and thaw the edamame under water and drain
3. Place the beans onto a baking pan or dish and then add olive oil over top of them,
4. *black peppers*
5. Bake for about 10 to 15 minutes until the crunchy.

References

http://www.nhlbi.nih.gov/health/public/heart/hbp/dash/new_dash.pdf

www.mayoclinic.com
www.mayoclinic.com/health/dash-diet-recipes

www.dashdiet.org
www.dashdiet.org.dash_diet_recipes

http://www.nhlbi.nih.gov/health/public/heart/hbp/dash/new_dash.pdf

www.webmd.com

www.doctoroz.com

www.medicalnewstoday.com

"The Dash Diet For Weight Loss" by Thomas J Moore

Lemon Thyme Orange Roughy
http://www.mayoclinic.com/health/healthy-recipes/NU00524

Quinoa Risotto

http://www.mayoclinic.com/health/healthy-recipes/RE00024

List of Dash Diet Recipes
http://www.mayoclinic.com/health/dash-diet-recipes/RE00089

Baldwin, A. (2012). *Transcript: Here's the Thing: Robert Lustig.* Retrieved 2013, from WNYC: http://www.wnyc.org/shows/heresthething/2012/jul/02/transcript/

Cole, R. (2008). *21 Day Sugar Detox.* Retrieved 2013, from Rosecole.com: http://www.rosecole.com/handouts/21DaySugarDetox.pdf

Dolson, L. (2008). *Fructose - Sweet But Dangerous.* Retrieved 2013, from About: http://lowcarbdiets.about.com/od/nutrition/a/fructosedangers.htm

Ford, A. (2013). *Why Do Women Love Sugar?* Retrieved 2013, from Divine Caroline: http://www.divinecaroline.com/self/wellness/why-do-women-love-sugar-truth-about-your-sweet-tooth

Gebel, E. (2011). *How the Body Uses Carbohydrates, Proteins, and Fats.* Retrieved 2013, from Diabetes Forecast: http://forecast.diabetes.org/magazine/features/how-body-uses-carbohydrates-proteins-and-fats

Healthy Living. (n.d.). *Glycemic Index.* Retrieved 2013, from Healthy Living 2008: http://www.healthy-living.org/html/glycemic_index_table.html

Jegtvig, S. (2013). *How Much Added Sugar Can I Eat a Day?* Retrieved 2013, from About: http://nutrition.about.com/od/askyournutritionist/f/howmuchsugar.htm

Kovaks, J. (2013). *How to Increase Your Metabolism and Start Losing Fat.* Retrieved 2013, from WebMD: http://www.webmd.com/diet/features/increase-your-metabolism-start-losing-fat

Mercola, J. (2010). *76 Dangers of Sugar to Your Health.* Retrieved 2013, from Dr. Mercola: http://articles.mercola.com/sites/articles/archive/2010/04/20/sugar-dangers.aspx

Moss, M. (2013). *The Extraordinary Science of Addictive Junk Food.* Retrieved 2013, from NYT: http://www.nytimes.com/2013/02/24/magazine/the-extraordinary-science-of-junk-food.html?pagewanted=all&_r=0

Repinski, K. (2011). *How Sugar Ages Your Skin.* Retrieved 2013, from Prevention: http://www.prevention.com/beauty/beauty/how-sugar-ages-your-skin

Rosedale, R. (2008). *Be a Fat Burner.* Retrieved 2013, from Healthy Living: http://www.healthy-living.org/html/be_a_fat_burner.html

SELF Nutrition Data. (2013). *Glycemic Index.* Retrieved 2013, from Self Nutrition Data: http://nutritiondata.self.com/topics/glycemic-index#glycemic

Toad. (2012). *How to Complete the 21 Day Sugar Detox with Ease.* Retrieved 2013, from Primal Toad: http://primaltoad.com/sugar-detox-tips/

Van Allen, J. (2013). *Kick Your Sugar Addiction .* Retrieved 2013, from Shine: http://shine.yahoo.com/healthy-living/kick-sugar-addiction-9-simple-steps-152600441.html

Natural Healing College Authors (2013) Alternative Medicine Treatments: The Holistic Health Practitioner seeks to take care of the root causes of disease, rather than merely eliminating or suppressing the symptoms

Voiland, A. (2012). *10 Things the Food Industry Doesn't Want You to Know.* Retrieved 2013, from US News and World Report - Health: http://health.usnews.com/health-news/articles/2012/03/30/things-the-food-industry-doesnt-want-you-to-know

WebMD. (2012). *Sugar Addiction: Symptoms, Cravings, Detox, and Diet Tips.* Retrieved 2013, from WebMD: http://www.webmd.com/diet/ss/slideshow-sugar-addiction

wiseGeek. (2013). *What is Metabolism?* Retrieved 2013, from wisegeek: http://www.wisegeek.com/what-is-metabolism.htm

Reference Books:

Alternative-Medicine -The-Definitive-Guide
-by-Larry-Trivieri-Jr-9781587611414
Anatomy-and-Physiology-for-Dummies
-by-Maggie-Norris-9780470923269
Ayurvedic-Cooking-for-Westerners-by
-Amadea-Morningstar-9780914955146
Ayurvedic-Yoga-Therapy-by
-Mukunda-Stiles-9780940985971
Becoming-Raw
-by-Brenda-Davis-9781570672385
Complete-Food-and-Nutrition
-Guide-by-Roberta-Duyff-9780470041154
Encyclopedia-of-Herbal-Medicine
-by-Andrew-Chevallier-9780789467836
Essentials-of-Anatomy
-by-Valerie-C-Scanlon-9780803622562
Fitness-and-Health
-by-Brian-Sharkey-9780736056144
Food-Cures
-by-Joy-Bauer-9781609613129
Foods-to-Fight-Cancer
-by-Richard-Beliveau-9780756628673
Healing-with-Vitamins
-by-Editors-of-Rodale-Health-Books-9781594868061
Internal-Cleansing
-by-Linda-Berry-9780761529323
Nutrition-for-Life
-by-Lisa-Hark-9780756626235
Prescription-for-Dietary-Wellness
-by-Phyllis-Balch-9781583331477
Prescription-for-Herbal-Healing
-by-Phyllis-Balch-9780895298690
Prescription-for-Nutritional-Healing
-by-Phyllis-Balch-9781583334003

Secrets-of-the-Pulse
-by-Vasant-Lad-9781883725136
Textbook-of-Ayurveda-Vol-1
-by-Vasant-Lad-9781883725075
Textbook-of-Ayurveda-Vol-2
-by-Vasant-Lad-9781883725112
http://www.whfoods.com/genpage.php?tname=faq&dbid=32#eating
The-Complete-Book-of-Chinese-Health-and-Healing
-by-Daniel-Reid-9781570620713
The-Herbal-Drugstore
-by-Linda-White-9781579547059
The-Herbal-Medicine-Makers-Handbook
-by-James-Green-9780895949905
The-Human-Body-Book
-by-Steve-Parker-9780756628659
The-New-Detox-Diet
-by-Elson-Haas-9781587611841
the-worlds-healthiest-foods
-by-George-Mateljan-9780976918547
The-Yoga-of-Herbs
-by-David-Frawley-9780941524247
Vitamins-Herbs-Minerals
-by-H-Winter-Griffith-9781555612634

Other Recommended Reads:

Books by Shawn Chhabra

http://www.amazon.com/Shawn-Chhabra/e/B00H90O8J8

The Dash Diet Weight Loss Solution: 2 Weeks to Drop Pounds, Boost Metabolism, and Get Healthy (A DASH Diet Book...

The DASH Diet Cookbook: Quick and Delicious Recipes for Losing Weight, Preventing Diabetes, and Lowering Blood...

The Everything DASH Diet Cookbook: Lower your blood pressure and lose weight - with 300 quick and easy recipes...

Weight Loss by Quitting Sugar and Carb - Learn How to Overcome Sugar Addiction - A Sugar Buster Super Detox Diet...

You've been provided with a perfect body to house your soul for a few brief moments in eternity. So regardless of its size, shape, color, or any imagined infirmities, you can honor the temple that houses you by eating healthfully, exercising, listening to your body's needs, and treating it with dignity and love.- Dr. Wayne Dyer

FREE RECIPE BOOK OFFER: Free Dash Diet Healthy Recipes Offer! with Free Mediterranean Diet Recipes!

PLUS, additional chapter: Simplified Detox!

(includes information about Detox, Cleansing Diet, Glycemic Index)

FREE Bonus Offer: free recipes and other health and wellness related books

Please Click Here for Instant Access to Free Recipe Book
http://www.healthylifenaturally.com/dashdiet/

One Last Thing

Writing a book that is packed with useful information requires time, commitment and dedication from the authors. If you enjoyed this book and found it useful I'd very grateful if you'd post a an honest review on Amazon. Your support really does make a difference and we read all the reviews personally.

Here is the link to leave a review. Thanks!

https://www.amazon.com/review/create-review?asin=B00HAVX3UQ

Healthy Life Naturally!

Printed in Great Britain
by Amazon.co.uk, Ltd.,
Marston Gate.